P9-DJU-901

An imprint of Simon & Schuster Children's Publishing Division
1230 Avenue of the Americas, New York, New York 10020
Copyright © 2011 by Lauren Bosworth

All rights reserved, including the right of
reproduction in whole or in part in any form.

SIMON & SCHUSTER BFYR is a trademark of Simon & Schuster, Inc.
For information about special discounts for bulk purchases, please contact Simon &
Schuster Special Sales at 1-866-506-1949 or business@simonandschuster.com.
The Simon & Schuster Speakers Bureau can bring authors to your live event. For
more information or to book an event, contact the Simon & Schuster Speakers
Bureau at 1-866-248-3049 or visit our website at www.simonspeakers.com.
Book design by Lucy Ruth Cummins
The text for this book is set in Caslon.
Manufactured in the United States of America
2 4 6 8 10 9 7 5 3 1
Library of Congress Cataloging-in-Publication Data
Bosworth, Lo, 1986–
The Lo-down / Lo Bosworth.
p. cm.
ISBN 978-1-4424-1200-2 (pbk.)
1. Dating (Social customs)—Juvenile literature. 2. Teenage girls—Psychology—
Juvenile literature. 3. Interpersonal relations—Juvenile literature. I. Title.
HQ801.B7675 2011
306.73—dc22
2010021499
ISBN 978-1-4424-1201-9 (eBook)

The names and some of the identifying details of people
mentioned in this book have been changed.

Pina

PiNA

LO BOSWORTH

SIMON & SCHUSTER BFYR

NEW YORK   LONDON   TORONTO   SYDNEY

For Mom and Dad,
loving each other since
March 18, 1978

ACKNOWLEDGMENTS

THERE ARE A NUMBER OF PEOPLE I'D LIKE TO RECOGNIZE FOR helping to make my first book a reality. First, my family and friends. You have all provided me with unwavering support. Next, a hug and a kiss for Scott for teaching me about true love. At Ellen Rakieten Productions, a thank-you to Hayley Lozitsky for such a brilliant idea. Max Stubblefield at UTA. A big thanks to Matthew Elblonk, my literary agent at DeFiore and Company. Meghan McPartland and Nicole Perez, PR czarinas at Rogers & Cowan. David Stanley and Carolyn Conrad, my hotshot attorneys at WWLLP. At Simon & Schuster (and just a general "thanks" here too for believing in me from the get-go): Alexandra Cooper (best editor ever), Lucy Cummins, Julia Maguire, Jenica Nasworthy, Justin Chanda, Anne Zafian, Paul Crichton, and Michelle Kratz. Thank you all so, so much.

INTRODUCTION

I SNAGGED MY FIRST BOYFRIEND IN THE FIFTH GRADE. IT WAS A thrilling relationship, full of shy glances in the elementary school hallway and love notes saying, "Check here if you like me, check here if you don't." A few months of hand holding later, sixth grade rolled around. And one day, out of nowhere, I decided that it was *over*. No real reason (do real reasons exist when you're eleven?), just a gut feeling. So I pulled the trigger, broke my first heart, and set out to find my next perfect match.

And that first relationship, and how it ended, describes all the relationships I would have for the next seven years. I graduated from high school as the ultimate man-eater. I had a hot boyfriend one day—and the next, gone! I liked to flirt, to play games, and to move on when the spark fizzled out. Experiencing zero to very little heartache was the easiest way for me to navigate the boy kingdom of Laguna Beach High School. Any normal person would think I was crazy, or boy crazy at least. And it was totally true.

What was really going on? I wasn't ready for a real relationship, so I created ones that were comfortable for me and ended them when things got too mushy. But I *knew* that I wasn't ready, and that's what made my flirtatious escapades different from a lot of girls my age.

Because a lot of girls my age *did* want a serious boyfriend. Their hearts ached for boys, and I saw far, far too many of them crushed by sixteen-year-old losers. It was through their pain that I decided to avoid all those icky, uncomfortable, make-your-bones-shake kinds of experiences. It was also through their pain (and a bit of my own: I did take a *few* guys more seriously) that my understanding of relationships grew.

It was when I left home for college that real relationships started to happen to me—or let's say, I opened my heart to them. Why the change of heart? Well, scientifically, I was becoming a woman, though it sounds a bit dorky to say. But truthfully, I was also very lonely away from home, and the girls at school just weren't cutting it in the friendship department. He was pretty much my best friend and my perfect other half. For the time being, at least. After two years, he moved home to Seattle, and that was that. I was totally, completely crushed and freaked-out. I was still very young, but when we were together I liked to imagine what my first name sounded like paired with his last name. I can't believe I just admitted that, but I have a sneaking suspicion that it's a pretty common thing to do.

So, from that point on I was hooked on relationships. I stopped looking at my friends from high school like they were bananas. I discovered that relationships are great, that they make you feel warm and fuzzy and fulfilled. At least, if they're good. And that's where this introduction makes a left turn into Sadville. A lot of relationships are *not* good ones. They suck! They make you feel like poo! And you don't deserve that.

I learned about really nasty relationships from a particularly foolish ex-boyfriend of mine. He was traditionally handsome and athletic, knew how to put the moves on chicks, and drove a nice car. I fell for him and he fell for me. He said I was different from any girl he had ever dated. So, why didn't it work out? In the long run, he wanted me to change . . . physically. I felt pressure from him to be hotter and skinnier and to dress skankier the entire time we were together. When we broke up, he actually had the balls to tell me that he was "used to dating girls who do double days at the gym" and that sometimes he didn't like the way I dressed. Excuse me, jerk. Stop right there. I've heard enough.

And so, for the next week, I kept telling myself that 120 pounds was thin enough for a girl my size and that *Vogue* likes my Chloé boots even if he doesn't, thank you very much! You get the picture. And it was from that messy experience that I learned the most valuable relationship lesson I have yet: It's not that I wasn't the right girl for *him*, he wasn't the right guy *for me*. I didn't, shouldn't, and will never change who I am for a guy. This isn't some ultra-feminist talking. It's just a basic human truth about being true to yourself. My future hubby will love me for me, and that's how it should be.

Hopefully, you feel the same way. If you don't, I'm going to get right to the point: You are approaching relationships the wrong way. You think it's okay to change who you are so that another person will like you? Does the version of you that he likes make the real you feel good about yourself? Probably not, now that you're really considering it.

If you're unhappy with yourself because you're fulfilling his needs rather than your own, how will you have a happy relationship? It's impossible! How do you change that? You incorporate *believing in yourself* into your relationship approach immediately. As in, right this second. Stand up for who you *already* are, because that person is more remarkable than you can imagine.

If you're already in a happy, lasting relationship, congratulations. It's clear that you know what makes you happy, and this relationship guide will give you a fabulous new perspective on your love life.

And if you're still on the hunt for your perfect mate, it's time to take the "I'll never find a boyfriend" frown off your face (it'll wrinkle faster if you stare like that, by the way).

All you have to do is continue to read all the juicy goodness I'm about to share with you and then enforce what we discuss in your own life. Trust me, sweetness, there is hope for you yet!

Lots and lots of love,

PART 1

DATING MISTAKES
AND RELATIONSHIP PITFALLS

I LIKE TO LISTEN TO THE POSTAL SERVICE'S SONG "SUCH GREAT Heights" when I think about happy people in relationships. When Ben Gibbard sings that people are "corresponding shapes like puzzle pieces from the clay," I picture how nicely a boy and a girl fit together when they hug. Her arms fit snugly under his, both pairs entwined around their bodies, her head cozying up right under his neck. People really do fit together like puzzle pieces.

Imagine yourself as a piece of this love puzzle. Pretend you are the left bottom corner, with two straight edges and one sort of wiggly side. Only one other piece joins up perfectly with your own. As an experienced puzzle solver, you know that it's just a matter of finding this mysterious missing piece, the one piece that fits just right, in order to complete your relationship puzzle.

We'll get to the part about finding this elusive matching piece, but for now let's focus on all of these mismatched ones and all the stuff that comes along with trying to pair up with them.

Now, when you put together a real puzzle, would you ever rip off a little section of your own piece just so that it would fit up against another? No way! You may be frustrated that you haven't found the corresponding shape yet, but you would never go so far as to mutilate your own piece of colored cardboard for another piece's benefit. Besides, your mom would probably yell at you for mangling her puzzle of the American flag or a Monet painting or whatever.

So, no. You wouldn't ruin your own piece just to complete the puzzle. That's crazy. So why, then, are you so willing to rip up your piece when it comes to your real life, your love life? Don't say you haven't done it. Every girl has torn her piece to shreds for the "perfect" guy. I've done it, and more than once.

I'll explain further. Sometimes you rip up your piece to match another in order to feel those initial moments of relationship bliss, hoping that in the long run your mismatched pieces don't feel too smushed together. Be cautious, my lovely friend. They soon will go from smushed to suffocating, no doubt about it.

Take an ex-fling of mine, for example. He was a rock-'n'-

roller, and I'm very musically challenged. I started listening to weird music and wearing studded bracelets to try to fit in with him. Not exactly *moi*. Let's just say it ended quickly, and apart from my return to stone-encrusted jewelry, it left me feeling down in the dumps.

So, aside from the inevitable messy breakup, what's the problem with mismatched puzzle pieces? When you change yourself in order to create a comfortable, fitting relationship *for him*, it's bound to fail from day one. Why? First and foremost, you are compromising who you really are for another person. Am I really a punk-rock-listening, studded-bracelet-wearing groupie? Absolutely not! Changing for someone else only discredits the incredible person you already are, and you should never allow anyone, especially *you*, to treat you with disrespect.

Second, when you're not yourself, you're bound to feel unhappy. Finally—and this is a no-brainer—no real relationship is able to survive on the aforementioned unhappiness and fakery, the results of self-compromise.

And anyway, why do you want a relationship with a guy who wants you to change? He's a shortsighted loser! Hello, you're awesome just as you are, and you deserve someone who appreciates that huge and important fact.

You're young, beautiful, classy, and smart. You have a good head on your shoulders and big dreams. Believing in the qualities you already possess and the person you already are is what is going to land you your perfect match. Why? Because guys respect and love women who love and appreciate themselves for who they really are.

Now, don't freak out when I say this: There are guaranteed to be some bumps along the way in your quest for the perfect boyfriend. Whatever you do, though, *believe in yourself.* It will change your love life forever, and for the better. If you fail to believe, well, trust me, all you'll end up with is a broken heart. You'll hurt yourself and allow others to hurt you. And I can't have any of my girls feeling down in the dumps. It's not a good look for you, just like blue nail polish, even OPI Russian Navy.

Now that I've explained why it's an excellent idea to have faith in your awesome self, let's get back to the bumps in the road. There will always be bumps in the relationship road! Until you find *the* guy, all your previous relationships really are just more and more bumps. The upside? You are guaranteed to learn more about why your puzzle piece is shaped the way it is and about the kind of person you need to find in order to create that perfect match.

QUIZ: DATING HISTORY

Before we really break into dating mistakes and relationship pitfalls, it's time for a quiz. This quiz is not here to give you the same side-eye that your teacher does when you're late to class. Its only function is to help you and me determine how much relationship experience you already have and what

i. A 2. B 3. B 4. D 5. C 6. B 7. C 8.

kind of experience it is. You could be choosing the wrong guys and just need some honest advice from a friend (me!!) to open up your pretty eyes to all the nice ones out there. Please choose one answer per question and answer honestly. If you don't, the work we're doing won't help you snag a sweetie for yourself.

1. You and Dan have been hanging out off and on for a few weeks. On Thursday he mentions that you should go with him to his friend's party the next night. On Friday, though, Dan is nowhere to be found—MIA and unreachable on his cell. You:

    a. Don't call or text him. You think he should call you, and instead you spend Friday night alone at home.

    b. Call him once and leave this message: "Dan, I never heard from you today. Wanted to let you know I'm seeing a movie with Molly instead of going to the party. Hope all is well. Talk soon."

    c. Call him twice, but he doesn't pick up. You text him at eight p.m. asking about his plans. He replies at midnight, writing, "Sorry, babe. Crazy day. Just getting out to the party now."

    d. Have your mutual friend ask Dan if he is going to the party. If Dan says yes, you show up to the party with a girlfriend in tow.

2. A cute guy from your history class asks you out on a date. When he shows up, he:
   a. Comes to the door to get you.
   b. Texts you to let you know he's there, and you go meet him in the driveway.
   c. Texts you to let you know he's there, and you reply, "Do you mind coming in? I'd like you to meet my parents/best friend/dog."
   d. Honks, and you sneak out without saying good-bye.

3. After a great first date with Kevin at a cool restaurant:
   a. The two of you go to a party that you suggest, to meet up with friends.
   b. You continue the date with something unplanned, like a coffee or a stroll down the boardwalk.
   c. He takes you home, but there's no good-night kiss.
   d. He takes you to "the Point" to make out.

4. Your boyfriend of six months is quite popular on Facebook. He doesn't give a relationship status in his profile, and a lot of friends (guys and girls alike) post on his wall. You know some of the people, but some random girls are making you suspicious. You:

a. Demand that his profile photo be a picture of both of you and that he change his status to "In a relationship with [fill in your name here]."

b. Hack into his profile to read all his messages, posts, and pokes to random chicks.

c. Simply ignore what's bothering you. It's just Facebook, right?

d. Ask him how he knows these girls, and broach the subject of the absent relationship status. If you ask him, maybe he would consider changing it to "In a relationship."

5. You accidentally slip up and hurt his feelings when you tease him about something private in front of his friends. You:

a. Apologize dramatically in front of the group.

b. Continue making the joke. He's a guy—he should be able to handle it.

c. Find a private moment and sincerely apologize to him. He accepts the apology, and you end up having a good night.

d. Get so upset with yourself over your slipup, you somehow end up being the victim.

6. Your boyfriend of four months has been in a crabby mood the past few days. You:

a. Ask him if you did something wrong and, if you did, what you can do to make the situation better. If you didn't do anything wrong, he'll probably tell you what's up anyway and appreciate you noticing that something was off.

b. Bitch back at him. He shouldn't treat you badly for no reason.

c. Let him chill out for a few days, then ask if he wants to hang out over the weekend.

d. Bug him incessantly about what's up. If something is wrong, you deserve to know.

7. A girl who you sort of know from school sends you a Facebook message about your boyfriend. In the message she writes, "I wanted to let you know my sorority sister Meredith hooked up with your guy at his frat party last week. I've been cheated on before, and I just had to tell you." How do you respond?

a. You don't. You delete the message and ignore it completely.

b. You immediately call your boyfriend and ask him if anything really happened with Meredith. He says no, and you believe him.

c. You speak to a close friend in Meredith's sorority. She also confirms they hooked up.

When your boyfriend denies it, you choose
to believe your girlfriend and break things off
with him.

d.   You ask your BF, and when he tells you that
yes, it happened, you choose to stay with him
because he was honest with you.

8. You really like Mark, and one night you decide on a
whim to get intimate with him. He:

a.   Tells his friends all the details, and a week
later you hear snickering about the size of
your rump when you walk by them at school.

b.   Calls you once or twice again afterward, but
then you drift apart.

c.   Continues to see you, but you know he
continues to see other girls on the side as
well.

d.   Talks to you about dating more seriously. He's
really into you and wants to make sure you
feel the same way.

THE RESULTS

Tally up your points based on the results below. Afterward,
we'll discuss what your score means.

1.   a-4, b-1, c-2, d-3
2.   a-1, b-4, c-2, d-3

3. a-2, b-1, c-4, d-3
4. a-2, b-3, c-4, d-1
5. a-2, b-3, c-1, d-4
6. a-1, b-3, c-2, d-4
7. a-4, b-2, c-1, d-3
8. a-3, b-2, c-4, d-1

WHAT YOUR SCORE MEANS
8–11 POINTS: YOU'RE DOING GREAT!

Congratulations, you are right on track to finding the perfect guy by being yourself. You are smart, and you understand not only guys but human nature on a basic level. You are able to apologize when you're wrong, and you can get yourself out of a bad situation. Your respectable amount of relationship knowledge comes from experiencing both good and bad partnerships. Go get 'em, girl!

12–16 POINTS: YOU HAVE SOME EXPERIENCE!

Okay, you are right where most girls your age are. You've dated guys and maybe had one or two longer relationships. Sometimes guys you like may take advantage of your kindness and you don't realize it. Other times you know you've been wronged and you give guys second chances who don't deserve them. Stick with me, sweetie pie. We'll weed out all the losers and snag you a guy who deserves your time and attention.

17-24: You're in the Thick of It!

Okay, girlfriend. You are in way, way too deep with some total tool bags. Any guy who treats you badly does not deserve third, fourth, and fifth chances just because he is cute. It's time to re-evaluate how you feel about yourself (trust me, you're worth a million bucks!), because it's the perception you have of yourself that signals to assholes that it's okay to treat you badly. This is a tough situation to be in, but if you're serious about finding the right guy, it'll be an easy battle from here on out.

24-32: You're Just Learning!

Don't let your high score scare you away from relationships and from believing in yourself. You happen to be in a very good position, because as a relationship novice you have the superempowering opportunity to learn the good things about guys and relationships from the very beginning. You need to remember that when you put yourself out there, you are still the most important person in the equation, no matter what. It's just like in the first *Sex and the City* movie when Samantha says to Smith, "I love you, but I love me more." Remember those wise words, honey, because they are true, true, true. There really are tons of guys who want to get to know you, so be sure to put the right version of You out there from the start.

So, now you know your score and where you stand when it comes to guys, relationships, and yourself. If you scored high, don't worry! It's girls like you who really love the idea of love, and your only mistake may be that someone else initially pointed you in the wrong direction. But that's what's so great about being a BYT (bright young thing). You always have time to make up for love lost! With each new relationship comes a fresh start. Isn't that a novel idea?

TYPES OF GUYS: THE BADDIES

So, we've all read the magazine articles that classify guys into certain categories. The Bad Boy, the Romantic, the Foreigner. You know the deal. Let's head into this territory right now.

Lots of different types showed up in the quiz you just took, some good and some bad. Were you able to recognize the types of guys and how some of them don't always treat you with the respect you deserve? For example, is the guy in Question 1 of the quiz (a) Can't-Commit Charlie or (b) Arrogant Adam? The answer is obviously Can't-Commit Charlie, though I'm sure Arrogant Adam makes an appearance too (Question 8, for you type-A girls who will go back to look). Can't-Commit Charlie is a type of guy we've all had experience with, and a common type of guy to look out for.

Let's start with the guys my girlfriends and I like to call the Baddies. They're called the Baddies because *they are bad for you*. I want to begin with the bad types of guys because I'm hoping that as you read about them, you'll start to connect the dots about situations within your own relationships. We're trying to put your puzzle together properly, remember? That requires looking at different guys you've already experienced. Chances are, some of the puzzle pieces you tried to squish against your own are listed below.

Before we jump in, though, a quick side note about type-casting. Bottom line, I'm not writing a book to bash all the guys in the world. That's pretty lame. I really love boys. I'm boy crazy, even. But I save my love for the nice ones, not the jerks.

Any guy who treats you badly does it in a way that is clear and easy to identify, as long as you know what signals to look for. And anyone who is knowingly hurting someone else deserves to be called out. My hope is that if on the off chance Can't-Commit Charlie/Needy Nick/Peter the Player reads this, instead of getting pissy he'll realize how mean he is capable of being and change his ways. Here's to hoping!

THE SCALE

Different types of guys deserve different kinds of grades. The better the guy, the better the grade. Just like in school. The scale ranges from letter grades A to F. Remember, these next few pages are going to resemble a sucky report card, but you'll read about the high-scoring guys very soon.

A GUY WHO EARNS AN A: MARVELOUS.

A GUY WHO EARNS A B: PRETTY COOL.

A GUY WHO EARNS A C: MEH.

A GUY WHO EARNS A D: SUPER MEH.

A GUY WHO EARNS AN F: ROTTEN TO THE CORE.

CAN'T-COMMIT CHARLIE

Charlie is a seemingly nice guy, has a great group of friends, and is probably one of the more popular guys at school. He has a lot of interests. Most likely, too many interests. He always has a girl he likes, and a lot of girls who like him, too. You notice that he has dated quite a few girls, and while they tend to not work out in the long run, Charlie is still pretty nice to all of them.

Charlie is the type of guy you strictly, strictly, strictly have fun with. Remember how, in my introduction to this book, I talked about just having fun with guys in high school? Charlie is this kind of guy.

He will probably take you on a date or two, or to prom, but do not expect anything long term or serious from Can't-Commit Charlie. It's not that he never wants to commit to a girl, it's just that he doesn't want to commit to anyone right now.

Also, Can't-Commit Charlie will probably indicate to you a desire to get more serious if you approach the fun in a smart, responsible way. Don't be fooled by this outta-left-field seriousness! In the long run, he will get bored with the relationship and return to his noncommittal ways. And you should *never* change who you are for Can't-Commit Charlie. If he can't commit, then why should you?

Grade: C

ARROGANT ADAM

Oh, Arrogant Adam. What a simpleminded fellow he is. Arrogant Adam is so full of himself, he cannot see the big picture. He doesn't see the good in other people because his head is so clouded with how amazing (and arrogant) he is. He has a hard time sharing other people's views on what is cool or what sucks, because his opinion is always the best. Take heed if you happen to share his view on something! He will immediately treat you like a star, but ditch you when you show a difference of opinion.

Arrogant Adam also has a jaded view of females. No doubt he has a picture in his head of who and what his perfect lady companion is, and this girl only lives in fantasyland. This is the type of guy who will want you to change something about yourself in order to live up to his very high, very ridiculous standards. Dump him immediately.

Grade: C-

CLOSED-MINDED CHRIS

See "Arrogant Adam." Bonus: Closed-Minded Chris is also hateful. He is a racist, a bigot, or both, and he doesn't mind letting everyone know. Watch out for hurtful jokes and snide comments. When should you ditch Chris? Ten minutes ago.

Grade: F

PREDICTABLE PAUL

Predictable Paul goes both ways. One version sucks and one version is a-okay. The lame version of Predictable Paul goes like this: He is set in his ways, and girls are turned off because of this. For example, he always takes girls to Olive Garden on the first date (gross). Always. He always calls you three days after your first date or, worse, he texts you instead. He seems to break up with a girl after a month. Don't fall for Predictable Paul, no matter how cute he is. He is stubborn and unimaginative, and doesn't like to get off his much-beaten path.

The nicer version of Predictable Paul goes like this: He is nice to you and cares about your interests. You have a lot of fun together at first, but then things start to get a little boring. You know each other so well that you fall into the same habits. This is not always bad, and a lot of people are comfortable with the things they already know and love. If you love Predictable Paul, you are probably Predictable Polly. To make your guy Unpredictable Paul for the night, research a fun date idea and spring it on him out of nowhere. He is bound to return the favor.

Grade: D or B-

NEEDY NICK

Nick is a mama's boy. Plain and simple. He doesn't give back as much as he takes from you. In fact, he probably sees any sort of neediness in you as a turnoff. Wake up, Nick! You're not the only one who requires a little help here and there.

Nick depends on you to make dinner reservations, come up with plans, and make lunch. If you live together, he probably needs you to do his laundry. All the things he needs you to do for him he is perfectly capable of doing himself. The problem? He has never taken care of these things himself, and it's going to be very tough to get him to start. Needy Nick will also be shocked if you chat with him about things *you* need him to do for you. His way of life is set in stone, and if you complain, then *you* are the crack in it. He will most likely be happiest with a girl who gives in to him and his ways. Are you that girl? No way!

Grade: C

TEXTING TOM

Texting Tom knows that communication is important. What he has to learn is that communication over the phone or in person is usually better than texting, at least when it comes to girls he is wooing. Tom should respect you enough to CALL YOU to ask you out. Maybe he's texting you because he is nervous or embarrassed, but that isn't really an excuse. If he is texting you and you'd rather chat on the phone, respond with a simple message: "I'm pretty busy. Can we talk on the phone?" He will most likely get the hint. It's better to get into a pattern of phone calls rather than text messages right from the beginning. It's a more personal and better way to discuss what's going on without confusion. I find that the tone of a text message can sometimes be misinterpreted, and that can lead to trouble.

For example, my boyfriend sometimes sends me messages that are much shorter and to the point than the thoughtfully written little notes I usually receive. At first I thought he was angry with me about something, but then I learned he was just superbusy at work.

So remember, if your guy has a job, the best he can probably do from nine to five is text or e-mail. Don't give him a hard time for that, but in general, texting is not the way to go.

Grade: C+

PETER THE PLAYER

Peter the Player will make you think you are number one, ignore you, and then just as quickly start texting you again. His partners in playership? His cell phone and his Facebook/MySpace/Twitter accounts.

Peter knows exactly how to make you feel special, because he does it to girls all the time. He has no problem picking up the phone to call you, taking you out on dates, and meeting your mom. He is a smooth criminal, stealing hearts all over the place! He treats you like gold in the beginning, because he knows that once a girl is swooning over him, he can then get away with blowing her off more easily. What's tough is that Peter isn't a psycho whose number-one goal in life is to treat you badly. He loves girls, but his problem is that he will never have eyes for only one. Because of this, he has devised a slick way to keep all his ladies wrangled in at once.

You can spot a player a mile away based on his cell-phone usage and his Internet social pages. If Peter is constantly on his phone, he most likely isn't talking to his mom. He is juggling the four different girls he is seeing, sending them sweet texts or else ignoring them to give his attention to someone new. If his Facebook wall is full of different messages from different girls and he always has new friends, watch out. He is probably friending every hot girl he sees and then sending her messages saying, "Have we met before?" or "Do we know each other?"

If all signs point to "Player at Play," please back away slowly. He may treat you nicely now, but he is bound to treat you like poo eventually. The worst part? You know that there are *always* other girls associated with him, and they're being treated the exact same way.

Grade: F

CHEAP-O OLIVER

Cheap-o Oliver is probably nice, but oh man! He worries about money. Cheap-o Oliver is the kind of guy who asks you to go dutch on your first date. This is a bad sign. Chivalry is not dead, guys. It is expected that a guy will pay for a girl the first three times he asks her out, no matter what.

If money is an issue—and this is something everyone should be sensitive to—choose dates that are less costly or free. Cheap-o Oliver can easily make you dinner and take you on a nice hike if there are financial issues.

Also, you may find yourself dating a Cheap-o Oliver if at first he pays for you, but then expects you to go splitsies on absolutely everything after that. You should take him out sometimes, but he should remember to do the same for you.

Grade: C-

FOREIGNER FABIO

Fabio is sexy, sexy, sexy. Maybe a little smelly, too. If Fabio is visiting the lovely U.S. of A., he's probably also very aware of his exit date. Sure, foreigners seem charming and, well, foreign, but chances are, if he quickly sweeps you off your feet, he's just trying to get lucky while on vacation. Think about it.

If Fabio actually lives in the United States, give him a chance, unless he is giving off clear signals that he deserves additional "Baddies" titles.

If you are the one on vacation and you happen to meet your

foreign Prince Charming, have fun but be careful. In fact, this applies to any guy while you're on vacation, not just those in far-off countries. Return home with your sanity, your dignity, and your heart intact.

Grade: C

BAD-BOY BRAD

Ladies, there's a reason they're called Bad Boys. They are, literally, bad boys. I'm not talking about guys who ride motorcycles, à la Brad Pitt. I'm referring more to the kinds of guys who tend to get in trouble with the law, their parents, their school, and their friends. Bad Boys are more than a little bit shady, and they always seem to have a chick by their side. They may lie, cheat, and steal and, even worse, do it to *you*. Why females find these dangerous traits mysterious and intriguing I have absolutely no idea.

Think they're sexy all you want, but from a distance, please. I'd hate to see you arrested alongside him just because you were in a "wrong place at the wrong time" situation.

Grade: D-

TYPES OF RELATIONSHIPS:
THE BAD ONES

The Baddies aren't just descriptions in a book or the antagonists you read about in your favorite stories. Unfortunately, they're very real and they will forever break sweet girls' hearts all over the place. Whether they stomped on your best friend's heart or your own, I'm without-a-doubt certain that you know a few of them. What sucks the most about dealing with a guy who treats you badly is the aftermath. You feel alone and bummed out, sort of like you are the only one out there who understands what you're going through.

Your friends and family comfort you, reassuring you that breaking up was actually the right thing to do. And it's true. Leaving a dysfunctional relationship behind is the first step a girl needs to take to get away from a guy who doesn't treat her the way she deserves to be treated. Whether the breakup is fresh and stings like a first-degree burn, or a few months have passed, it's still an embarrassing and hurtful position to be in.

Being dumped, or doing the dumping, (if you did the dumping, good for you; if you were dumped, good riddance!) is no fun at all. We've all been there, and most of us will go through it again. Experiencing that "I'm all alone" feeling is total misery, so instead of letting you mope yourself, I'd like to introduce you to some of my friends and their personal experiences with some of the baddest Baddies out there.

Meet Catherine, Jillian, and Rachel. They are all beautiful, strong, smart women. If some of their experiences sound familiar to you, it's because they probably are! My friends are just like yours, each with their own ex-boyfriend. Here are their stories, along with a story of my own.

CATHERINE AND RYAN

Catherine is the most beautiful girl-next-door you'll ever meet. She has one of those button noses that is absolutely to die for, and long blond hair that she likes to wear in loose curls. She is girly beyond belief, her bedroom decked out in soft shades of pink and cream. Boys love Catherine. Sure, for her looks, but mostly because of the delightful personality that comes along with them. She loves to have fun and knows how to make people feel special. One of Catherine's best traits is that she takes care of the people she loves regardless of the situation. Catherine is a girl's best friend.

She met Ryan, a scruffy but handsome tough guy, in high school. No initial sparks, though: Ryan ran in a crowd that Catherine wasn't completely comfortable with. It was after graduation, when they both wound up moving to the same city, that they connected for the first time. They bumped into each other at a restaurant and, both feeling lonely and glad to see a familiar face, started up a conversation.

Catherine noticed that he was thoughtful and funny, not like the bad boy she had known from a distance growing up. She had never been out on a real date before, and when he asked her to dinner and a movie she immediately said yes. From the first date forward, Catherine and Ryan were virtually inseparable. He loved the way she took care of him, and she loved that someone could love her so much.

On a balmy Saturday night, the pair met up with some of their new friends at a popular restaurant. Ryan ordered a beer, and then another. Catherine noticed but didn't start to worry until his fifth drink. It was at that point that Ryan began to get louder and a little too easygoing, especially with strangers at the next table over. Because he was drunk, he misinterpreted what a man sitting across the way had said to him. In a second, Ryan became infuriated and snapped. What started as a great night out with friends ended in a fight and an assault charge.

Catherine was horrified at Ryan's behavior. She had heard stories about Ryan fighting in high school, but when they started dating, she pushed them to the back of her memory. In an instant those memories came flooding back, and she felt foolish for buying into his nice-guy persona.

Ryan bought her roses and surprised her with a home-cooked dinner the very next night. He apologized, saying he thought he had grown out of that stage and that he needed her help. Catherine was angry, but after hearing his story she began to soften. She was always eager to help her friends, and if her boyfriend, the guy she loved, needed help, then she would do whatever it took.

They continued dating without incident until one afternoon, a month later, Ryan came to her apartment in the middle of the day acting totally belligerent. He had driven there and was clearly under the influence of . . . something. Catherine was upset. After all the support she had given him, there he was, out of control again.

When he sobered up, he apologized immediately. He said it was a relapse and that she had done so much to help him. He said he loved her. He said he needed her. He said that he didn't know what he would do if she left. So she stayed. She loved Ryan back, even though the appearances from the Ryan she fell in love with were few and far between.

Finally, when Ryan didn't come home for two days, Catherine snapped. He didn't call her or send any kind of message that he was safe. After the countless times that Catherine had gone out of her way to let her boyfriend know that she cared, he couldn't be bothered to pick up a phone and return the favor. Drugs and alcohol were Ryan's true loves. Catherine was simply a fallback, someone he'd go to to feel like everything would be all right.

It wasn't an easy breakup. Ryan continued to push her for help, saying that she was the only person who loved him, the only one who could change him for good. Catherine, on the other hand, took the two DUIs and various assault charges he had racked up during their time together as a sign of the opposite. She realized that she was being taken advantage of by a person who was in need of professional help, not of a young girlfriend. She decided to leave him, and she left him for good.

JILLIAN AND TOMMY

Jillian is what many would describe as the perfect girlfriend. She is cute, with a shoulder-length haircut that shows off her shiny brown hair. Her apartment is always clean and decorated perfectly, the sea-grass rug perfectly complementing her beige couch and navy chairs. Jillian is an excellent cook, able to whip up anything from a breakfast burrito to a double-chocolate layer cake on a whim. She went to Berkeley and has an enviable job as a junior development exec at Warner Brothers.

Perfect, perfect, perfect. And Tommy knew it right off the

bat. He had been looking for a girl like Jillian for years, and finally he had found her. They met at Bar Chloe in Santa Monica, after one of her friends recognized a friend of his own and the group hung out all night. Jillian and Tommy's attraction was instant, and they kept eyeing each other until they couldn't stand to not speak any longer.

Just as she seemed to him, Tommy seemed perfect to her. He had olive skin, dark hair, and green eyes. She had always loved this combination in a guy—tan skin with light eyes. He was a few years older than she was (older = willing to commit), had graduated from UCLA (smart), worked as an investment banker at Morgan Stanley (could afford a family), and had grown up in Northern California near Berkeley (where she had gone to school). Jillian had high standards when it came to dating, and everything about Tommy added up perfectly on paper. He fit her list of must-haves to a T: smart, serious, great job, handsome.

They hit it off, each enraptured by the other. At the end of the night, Tommy asked for Jillian's phone number. She was excited but reasonable. She had given a lot of guys her number before, and a lot of them never called. She left the bar with her girlfriends, and as they were walking toward a cab her phone began to vibrate in her purse. She pulled it out, and though she didn't recognize the number, she answered anyway..

A familiar voice said, "Turn around," and she did. There was Tommy, standing on the sidewalk about twenty feet behind her. Grinning mischievously, he continued, "I know we just met, and I know I should wait the standard three days before calling you, but I can't help it. Dinner tomorrow?" Jillian, amazed at her luck, giggled flirtatiously and responded, "I can't believe it took you even that long to ask me."

After a whirlwind three months of dating, Tommy asked Jillian to be his girlfriend. At month five, he asked her to move in with her. On their first anniversary, he asked her to be his bride.

Jillian was ecstatic. Apart from a few minor fights and incidents, mostly around the time they moved in together, she knew she had found the One. What was even better to her was that she knew she was the One for Tommy, too.

Just when they were beginning to plan their wedding, Tommy was promoted at Morgan Stanley. The new job was better paying and more prestigious but required Tommy to travel five days out of the month. Jillian shook it off, understanding that the stipulation came with the territory and that he was still hers on all those other days.

The traveling began to take its toll on their relationship. Five days turned into seven, then into ten. Jillian's girlfriends made an effort to spend time with her while Tommy was gone, but she wasn't the same girl they had always known. Her bubbly personality was dimmed, and she worried that the time apart would cause long-term problems. She explained to her friends that when Tommy returned from his trips, he was tired and despondent rather than thrilled to be home with her. She would plan big dinners for his arrival, and he would eat in silence before crawling into bed.

She understood that everyone had bad days, but Tommy was taking it to a totally new level. She suggested finding a new job, getting a puppy, painting the living room—anything to change Tommy's outlook. Finally, they mutually decided on a trip to Cabo San Lucas to pull them out of their funk.

The night before their vacation, Tommy decided to spend an evening out with his friends. Jillian was thrilled that he was making an effort to have a little fun, and she happily encouraged him out the door. He and his friends were going to dinner at Dan Tana's, and he'd be home after that. Around eleven p.m., she got a text from Tommy that said, "Baby, we're going to a bar. My cell phone is dying. I love you." At this point, she had been hoping Tommy would be ready to come home to her, but she decided to be happy for him instead and got into bed.

She woke up at seven, looked around for her fiancé, and was frantic to find that he wasn't there. She called his cell phone only to have it go straight to voice mail. She called again. Same thing. After ten minutes of terrifying thoughts about her husband-to-be passing through her head, Tommy rolled through the front door. He had such a happy look about him that when he explained his phone had died and they stayed out so late he slept on his buddy Eric's couch, she brushed aside his night of fun as just that—a night of fun.

Two hours later, they left for LAX and got on their flight to Cabo. Just as expected, the hotel and beach were absolutely stunning. They shared romantic dinners, slept in every day until ten, and went big-game fishing on a huge boat with another couple they had met at the hotel. Tommy seemed happy and carefree, and he reconfirmed for Jillian how much he loved her. He explained that his job was taking its toll on him but that he knew if he stuck it out a few more months, the traveling would come to an end with a promotion to follow.

When they touched down in LA, Tommy announced that he didn't have the keys to their house. Jillian was befuddled. Had he locked them in the house or forgotten them in his car?

"No," he said quickly. He told her that one of Eric's friends, Melissa, had them, and she was supposed to have left them in their mailbox. The butterflies in Jillian's stomach fluttered as she nervously asked him who Melissa was and why she had his keys. He told her that he had left them in her car accidentally the night before their vacation.

"But you stayed at Eric's?" Jillian responded. He said that he had, but that they had met up with some girls and gone out with them after dinner. Melissa was their designated driver for the night.

"If she was driving, why didn't you have her take you home at the end of the night?" Jillian asked. He mumbled a response, something about wanting to spend time with his friends, the drive being too far, blah blah blah.

They spent the taxi ride home in silence, and when they arrived, he quickly grabbed the keys out of the mailbox. Tommy didn't seem comfortable the following days, and after playing their conversation over and over again in her head, Jillian asked Tommy once again about that night.

After a period of uncomfortable silence, Tommy came clean about what happened that night. He had gone out to dinner with his friends but had gone home with Melissa. He had cheated on Jillian, his perfect fiancée, with a strange girl he met out at a bar. He told Jillian he was so sorry, his depression caused him to do it, and he would take it back in a second if he could. He hoped that because he was being honest they could move on, that he hadn't meant to hurt her.

Despite his pleading, Tommy had hurt Jillian. He had spent the night with another woman, and she could never forgive him. In exchange for mere moments of pleasure, he had subjected his fiancée and family to embarrassment, hurt, and pain beyond belief. His series of mistakes that night took his perfect relationship with Jillian off its pedestal and reduced it to rubble.

"Why did you do it?" she demanded. He stumbled through an explanation—that he was down on himself because of his job and that the appeal of instant pleasure had been intoxicating. He said it was a release from his real life. *Sure, his real life with me,* she thought painfully.

Nothing Tommy could say would save what he had destroyed,

and Jillian immediately broke off their engagement. Tommy moved out of their house at her request the very next day.

So, what happened between Tommy and Jillian, the couple perceived to be perfect and problem free? It truly was Tommy's job that prompted him to stray, but blaming his work situation for his dalliance was uncalled for. Everyone is absolutely in control of his or her personal situation, and Tommy had countless opportunities to change his and save his relationship. Instead of finding a job that made him happier, a schedule that made him happier, and a life that made him happier, he stayed in his situation because it was expected and comfortable. He didn't have to go home with Melissa, but selfishly, he did.

The mistakes Tommy made come back to his ability to choose, and his bad choices piled on top of one another until they imploded. He chose work over his relationship with Jillian. Out of frustration and to relieve his stress, he chose another woman over his fiancée. He continued to knowingly choose what was wrong for his relationship over what was right, and he paid for it in the end.

RACHEL AND MARCO

Rachel and Marco had been friends for years before they began dating. It even took a few years of flirting between them before they actually decided to start seeing each other. From an outsider's perspective, they were perfect for each other. Marco had a sort of Johnny Depp look going, rode a motorcycle around town, and was a very smooth talker. For Rachel, though, the real clincher was that he was in a band.

She was completely enthusiastic about music. She loved going to all kinds of shows with her friends and, considering her looks fall into the drop-dead-gorgeous category, she got lots of attention from the bands. She knew how to let loose, make friends, and come off as totally carefree. Guys loved this about Rachel, and she knew exactly when to live it up.

So, the rocker and the beauty began to date. They understood each other, how both of their pasts influenced the kind of people they were now. They got to know each other's families, and their understanding of each other grew stronger.

As relationships always do, theirs started out smoothly. Marco would pick Rachel up on his bike, and they would disappear together for days. They went on adventures, did outrageous things, and truly began to care deeply for each other.

Soon, the days and nights they spent together were few and far between. In the same way he used to disappear with Rachel by his side, he would evaporate from plain sight on his own. Rachel started to become accustomed to his comings and goings, attributing them to his lifestyle and his past. Marco was indeed mysterious, but it was a part of him that turned her on.

When he showed up again, they would pick up where they had left off and fall back into their old pattern. Rachel justified this by telling herself that she didn't want a boyfriend, simply a cool guy to have fun with. What she didn't realize, however, was that this was how Marco felt about relationships with women, period. He didn't want a commitment of any kind, regardless of how strongly he felt about a girl. He thought he was born to be free, and as long as Rachel didn't seem bothered by this, he would continue to date her in the same way.

Time passed, and despite Rachel's head telling her to keep it light, her feelings for Marco grew. It's natural that the longer you date someone, the more you fall for them. It's why so many people who date for years end up together in the long run. Rachel fell into this category, but Marco didn't. She did want a long-term relationship eventually, with the right person. She knew that she could really fall for him seriously, as long as he wanted to fall in love with her. But he didn't. As much as he liked her, as much as they were right for each other, his fear of commitment continually stopped him.

Their relationship began to sour as Rachel, not wanting to be turned down, kept her desire to grow their relationship to herself. Marco continued to keep it light between them, despite sensing that Rachel was beginning to want more.

Rather than discussing what they each really wanted, they began to hurt each other. Out of anger, Rachel would see other people when Marco disappeared. When he found out, he would see other women to get back at her. It was an endless cycle of betrayals followed by reconciliation.

Finally, Rachel came clean about her desire for an official relationship with Marco. She said he owed it to her, that he should respect and love her enough to make her his girlfriend. He turned her down, saying that he was honest about his feelings from the beginning and that it wouldn't work out if they were a real couple. He said that what they had together was good exactly the way it was.

In reality, what Marco meant was that he was happy seeing her as long as she never came first. If she was never his girlfriend, he didn't owe her anything and·could continue to see her on his terms. Unfortunately, blinded by her love for him, she agreed to continue dating. She hoped that if they continued spending time together, they would end up together. She went with her heart and figured that simply dating Marco was better than no Marco at all.

What finally broke Rachel and Marco up for good? Another fight, this one bad enough that it caused Marco to seriously date another woman simply out of spite. As Marco's new girlfriend flittered about in front of her eyes, Rachel realized the truth about her years-long relationship with Marco. He would never commit to her, no matter what she endured or who she was. Rachel knew he was dating another girl simply for show. He wanted to hurt her, and for no reason other than the fact that Rachel had had enough of him.

So, she moved on, finally understanding that Marco was simply not right for her, even though she had cared for him. She wanted a commitment, and he didn't. And because she wanted it, she owed it to herself to find someone who felt the same way.

ME AND JOHN

We met a few weeks after I broke up with my previous boy-friend. My best friend, Amanda, was dating John's best friend, and she thought we might be a good match. Amanda knows that I tend to fall for the tall, dark, and handsome kind of guy, and John fit into that mold perfectly. We met for the first time at the UCLA vs. USC football game, and there was an instant attraction between us. The group of us ended up spending the whole weekend together, which I took as a very good sign.

I definitely had initial reservations about John. He grew up in LA, and considering that I had lived in the city for a few years, I was familiar with many of his previous conquests. The stories about him poured in from girlfriends and acquaintances. I listened to them all describe him as a huge player with a very healthy amount of self-esteem. But the only side I had seen of him so far was incredibly sweet and thoughtful—so, instead of listening to my friends' warnings, I ignored them.

When we started dating more seriously, John actually brought up his reputation. He said that people were always talking about him and that the majority of the stories I had heard were coming from psycho ex-girlfriends. He openly admitted to cheating on past girlfriends, but he promised that with me, it would be different.

And I ate it up. It was out of my own narcissism that I believed him. I had turned players into perfect boyfriends before, and I thought that my experience with John would be the same. Looking back at this encounter, I realize now that my ego took hold of the normal functions of my brain as I moved forward into a relationship with him. Turns out, my train of thought that day officially goes down as one of the more moronic moments of my life.

As we continued dating, there were great days with John and terrible days with him as well. When we had fun together, we had So. Much. Fun. When he got into one of his moods, which was frequent, it was like tiptoeing around someone else's bratty five-year-old. You don't know what will set the kid off further, and you don't know what to do to calm him down. This was our cycle: up and down, up and down.

To make matters worse, his incessant text messaging, which I brushed off for months, started to bug me. Who was so important that he had to be in constant communication with them? I tried and tried to rationalize that he was busy making contacts in his search for a job postgraduation, but it just wasn't so. On the rare occasion he set his phone down, the screen would be cluttered with different messages, all from senders with female first names.

Our issues eventually grew from bothersome to personal. John had been a college athlete, a baseball player whose days had, since childhood, begun with exercise and ended with Muscle Milk. He was vigilant in his routine and became clearly perturbed when I wasn't consistently willing to join in on the sweaty fun. If I mentioned a run I had gone on or a yoga class I'd attended, his smiles quickly turned to questions like, "Well, how long did you run for?" or "Why didn't you do that yesterday, too?" That I didn't match his daily workouts and lifestyle routine sincerely bothered John and left me feeling inadequate and downright fatty, fat, fat. I could only take so much criticism without feeling hurt, especially when I was satisfied with the way I was living my life.

As I started to crack, John became fed up with me. I would get angry and have a hard time expressing to him what was wrong, mostly out of sheer embarrassment. He was saying things to me that caused a lot of pain and hurt, continually reenforcing his underlying belief that something about me just wasn't good enough for him.

As backward as it sounds, I now realize that internalizing the abuse from him again comes back to my own ego. I got myself into a relationship with a well-known player, and I thought I could handle it. I thought that if I didn't allow myself to be distressed, or at least to show that I was irritated by things that went wrong, then I would have the relationship I desired with John in the end.

Finally, John snapped. He went on vacation with his friends and told me that in order for him to properly think about our relationship, he wouldn't be able to speak to me while he was gone. I agreed but was extremely frustrated by this. He routinely exploded when I couldn't tell him why I was upset, and now he was doing it back to me. So eight days passed with very little contact from him. That's right. Eight days. The longest I'd ever remained silent was for thirty minutes.

When he returned, he didn't have much to say. More than a week of sunning himself and he still couldn't figure out which way he wanted our relationship to go? I was livid, and I made my decision based on having endured the silent treatment for too long. It was over between John and me, and all that was left was for me to tell him.

When we broke up, we talked for a long time. I told him it didn't turn out how I had expected it would between us. I needed more of a commitment from him, and he, despite the wholesome relationship he told me he desired, wasn't willing to follow through. For John, there was always someone or something else more important to him than I was. His friends, random chicks, or parties always came first. I was simply an afterthought, a blip on the radar, once he realized I wasn't the perfect girl he'd envisioned for himself.

To this day I tell myself that I should have known better. He was my first real mistake, and because of the way I was treated, he will be my last. Everyone has to learn their lesson about bad relationships from somebody, though, in order to move on to great ones, and I learned my lesson about bad guys from John.

A few weeks later, after I had played out the collapse of my relationship in my head over and over again, I at last came to peace with it. I realized it wasn't anything that I had done, and that I couldn't have done anything differently to save it. No amount of exercise would have made him stick around, as in reality he had manipulated inconsequential things that bothered him as a way to rationalize treating me badly, as a reason to get out. What John desired at the beginning—a healthy relationship—is what I participated in but what he failed to follow through on. It wasn't me. It was him.

Before John, I didn't have enough negative relationship experience to be clued in to this. But after John, I had to come to this realization on my own in order to move on. It's the best relationship truth I have discovered yet: When your relationship falls apart, you have to understand that he just isn't the right guy for you, *not* that you must not be the right girl for him. If you think that you were the one who needed to change or act differently, your ex has control over your self-esteem and your psyche. You have to break down this power structure and believe in what *you* know to be the truth. By doing this, you will have the energy and dignity to move forward into stronger, healthier relationships. That is what I did and what gives me the ability to share this truth with you as well.

DO YOU SEE A PATTERN?

As you read my story and the stories of my girlfriends, do you see a pattern in them? Every one of our relationships ended, but why? My friends and I are different, as is each guy. A pattern exists, though, and it's a pattern attributable to the behavior of my friends and me in every situation.

What's the pattern? We ignored a telltale sign or feeling in the relationship that indicated trouble of some kind. It's a common mistake, and the mistake I made in my relationship could be thought of as one of the worst.

Why do women make this mistake? It's simple, really. They are so entranced by their guy, their relationship, whatever, that signs of problems are brushed under the rug in favor of existing bliss. Women, and men for that matter, do this because feeling good is so much better than feeling bad. More often than not, people would rather continue feeling blissful than hit the brakes and examine something that gives them an uncomfortable feeling.

Desiring happiness over having awkward conversations doesn't make you careless, it's just human nature. The way to rise above evolution, though, is to avoid relationships with people you immediately get warning signs from and to end relationships with people who give off signs once you get to know them better.

On a different note, every relationship (with a Baddie or a nice guy) will face problems that in fact *don't* resemble blazing red stop signs. Frequently these more minor issues are easily fixed if examined. So if something pops up, stop being paranoid about being paranoid and speak up. It's important to address issues as they happen instead of ignoring them. If you do, chances are the issue will dissipate and you can continue on happily, content that you've put whatever It is to rest. If you don't, you feed the issue. And if you feed it, it grows, until it becomes the reason that your relationship is coming to an end.

Let's identify the reason, or indicator, from each story that my friends and I ignored. In every case, if the signs had been dealt with rather than ignored, the outcomes might have been different.

Catherine ignored the sign that Ryan loved alcohol more than he loved her. He took her for granted, and she endured months of pain before she dealt with the obvious in an appropriate way. He was a Needy Nick all the way. Jill saw how Tommy's persona changed drastically when work didn't go his way. Rather than push him to change his situation for the better, she mired in it until it got the best of her. Rachel failed to hold Marco accountable when he disappeared: She didn't do or say anything about it. Marco seemed capable of combining every sort of nasty Baddie trait simultaneously. Finally, I ignored John's long string of previous messy relationships. He was an obvious Peter the Player, and I mistakenly thought that I would be the exception to his rule.

In every case, my friends and I had the opportunity to change the situation, and we failed to do so. We were dating douche lords. All the signs pointed to "dating a Baddie," and we took notice but continued on anyway. We should have left the relationships for better ones at that point, but instead we allowed them to run their course and ended up hurt and miserable. We should have stuck up for ourselves when we had the chance, but we didn't. Lessons have been learned, though, and that's the reason I'm writing this guide: to help you learn from the mistakes of others in order to avoid them for yourself.

Perhaps you have fallen into the same pattern my friends and I did. Maybe you've ignored a sign that indicates you are dating the wrong guy for *you*. To help you figure it out, try writing out the story of your own relationship. You'll most likely stumble upon the sign if you haven't already. Once you realize it, identify that you aren't the first girl to make that mistake, and feel better that we're moving into positive relationships from this point on.

The following questions and prompts will help you:

- What does he do that upsets you most?
- Is there something about him that initially made you uncomfortable but that you've brushed aside?
- It's hard to forgive him when he . . .
- When have you been happiest with him, and why?
- When have you been the most down over him, and why?
- Has he done something to break your trust that you've forgiven him for anyway?

PART 2

BELIEVING IN YOURSELF

SO, YOU'VE HAD A FEW UNSUCCESSFUL RELATIONSHIPS. MAYBE the guys you've dated have never even been elevated to official boyfriend status. Clearly, something is missing or something always ends up going wrong. You continue to find yourself stumped, wondering why that great connection with a cutie frequently packs up its bags after a few weeks and hits the road. Sayonara, peace, ciao!

It's a frustrating situation to be in. You get your hopes up, you get comfortable, and then you start to see small cracks in the relationship. At this point, whether you're the one who breaks it off or if he's the one who does the dirty work, the result is never fun, and it always leaves both people feeling sort of . . . discouraged.

You wonder, *Where did I go wrong?* Maybe you didn't do something to turn him off, but maybe you did. Chances are, if you did, it probably wasn't coming from a true version of yourself. And that's where a lot of girls run into issues with relationships.

When you first hit it off with a guy, it's totally normal to have some jitters. What if my breath smells? Do these shoes match my outfit? Does he think my room is too messy? These kinds of thoughts are normal, funny, whatever. They are common, and these kinds of worries are totally okay.

It's when girls start to worry about the following kinds of statements that they get themselves into trouble: Am I funny enough? Am I prettier than his last girlfriend? Does he think I'm smart? I hope he doesn't think I'm a little heavy right now. I hope he thinks I have enough money to date him. I hope he thinks I'm good enough.

Now, think for a second. Be honest with yourself about the things I just wrote. Have you ever thought some of these things about yourself? Most likely, the answer is a definite yes. It's a vain part of human nature to idealize what you think you are *not*. But it's what you aren't that makes you who you are.

This is the reason I've written this book. To help you focus on who you already are and to love and appreciate this person. And to show you that the best guy for you is one who loves your self-confidence, who loves you for you.

Finding a guy who is able to love you for who you already are is very powerful—for both people involved in the relationship. When he respects you, you owe him that respect back. Because he loves the person you are, you won't ever feel undervalued or feel pressure to conform to some crazy goddess standard. He wants you to believe in yourself, and that kind of support feels good. That kind of support blossoms into love.

In addition, believing in yourself allows you to trust in the relationship lesson I've learned from my own experiences with boys, which, as it so happens, is the guiding light of this entire book. In fact, it's this guide's Golden Rule.

THE GOLDEN RULE

The Golden Rule teaches you to understand that if it doesn't work out with a guy, *he is not the right guy for YOU*, so ditch the misconception that *you must not be right for HIM*.

We're changing the power structure here, lovies, and it's in your favor. No more of this "he's just not that into you" nonsense. You're in charge of you and your relationships, and the perfect guy for you will fit into *your* life in a mutually beneficial way. The best part of the Golden Rule is that it is reflective of reality, not some heartbroken girl's version of what's right. The G.R. is real and it creates healthy, lasting relationships, as long as you allow yourself to believe in it. And to do that, you must first believe in yourself.

Let's talk about this idea of believing in yourself and how

it applies to romantic relationships. Let's say you worry that when you meet a guy he'll think you aren't funny enough and that maybe you could lose five pounds. It's these personal, internal worries women feel will make or break a new relationship. They believe that a guy will only like them if they are the ideal woman: smart and sexy. The trouble is, the thought process men and women use to come to what the image of the ideal woman is, is different. Females have an image in our heads of who we want to be, and males see us for who we already are.

Consider a woman getting ready to go out on a date with her boyfriend. Her cutie is waiting while she finishes dressing, and when she looks in the mirror she is slightly disappointed. She wanted to be Wonder Woman tonight for her guy, and the sexy red dress and flowing curls didn't turn out as she hoped. Her guy, however, is struck by his beautiful girlfriend, completely blown away by how special she looks. Understand the disconnect between men and women now? You may stare in the mirror and hope for something different. He sees the real you looking into that reflective piece of glass, and he loves that girl.

So, understand that if they've asked you out, it's because they are already into you. Did you read that correctly? If they've asked you out, it's because they are *already into you*! It's as simple as that, and it's your personal struggles with who you feel you should be that frequently make your exciting new relationship go down the toilet. Why? Because believe it or not, people tend to accidentally highlight the things they don't like about themselves. You don't think you're funny enough for him, so you try extra, super hard to be the coolest girl ever with self-deprecating humor and five too many jokes. You think you could lose a few, and so you only order salads when you're out with him, and he notices (and thinks you should start feeding yourself real food). *The cool, fun, sexy image you're trying to create is doing the opposite: It's highlighting your insecurities.*

Who wants to date a girl who's trying to fake it, when the girl he really likes is sitting right in front of him, too afraid to be herself and in reality, get the guy.

What does this all boil down to? It's about fear of rejection. Being turned down is embarrassing and hurtful, and it only leads you to wonder further about your insecurities, forever blaming them for your relationship mishaps. As it turns out, fear of rejection and personal insecurities go hand in hand, but this is something you can change. You can control your insecurities by understanding them. Once you do that, rejection becomes far less personal and far less hurtful.

So, how do you do that? First, you acknowledge that at the end of the day you cannot really control whether a guy likes you or not. Everyone has a different idea of what's attractive. But remember the Golden Rule! If it doesn't work out, he is just not the right guy for *YOU*. Don't fool yourself into believing the opposite. And if he's just not that into you, realize that *he really isn't valuable enough to stress over.*

On the upside, if he does like the person you are and in return you appreciate him, then you have found something special! If it turns out that he likes you for who you really aren't, you'll run into trouble. You are in control of the person you put out there, and as long as it's your true self, the chances of having a blissful relationship based in reality rather than dreamland are far, far greater.

Second, in order to control your fear of rejection you must take a look at what you're insecure about and why. Once you have done that and you understand the place you are coming from, it's much easier to move into a happier state. When you take a hard look at yourself, it can be extremely helpful to focus on all the things that are unique about you and the things that you really do love about yourself. It sure turns what you feel insecure about into small potatoes when you are able to get a sense of how special you are in reality. Whenever a guy is interested in you, remember that! He sees you as you really are, and if he asks you out, it's because he appreciates the real you.

If it takes a little time to meet the perfect guy, acknowledge that it isn't time wasted. It's time you are investing in yourself. It's guaranteed that you will be happier alone as you really are, than with a guy but faking it. The perfect guy will come along, and if you insist on entering into the relationship by presenting your true self to him (aka by following the Golden Rule), you are guaranteed to find love.

QUIZ: SO, WHO ARE YOU?

Yes, friends. It's that time again. I'm feeling a superfun, incredibly insightful quiz coming on. It will be gloriously full of adjectives, and all about you. That's right. We are moving into the sections of this book that are all about *you*, instead of all about *him*. At the end of the day, that's what this is about, right? You.

Get used to it, sister. *You* are the most amazing person in your own life, so let's utilize what your mama gave you to the fullest.

The quiz you are about to take will focus on how you handle day-to-day scenarios, important events in your life, and your friends and family. What you do and how you act says quite a bit about the kind of person you are, but also about your maturity level. Bottom line, the more mature a woman is, the better equipped she is to handle a serious relationship with a man. Maturity is about self-awareness and self-sacrifice, but not about less fun. Some of the most mature people I know are also the wildest, but they understand their priorities and how everything falls into place.

I'm ready to start quizzing, are you? To better build the bond between us, I'm going to let you know which answers I picked at the end. That way, if you aren't always picking what you think are best answers, you won't feel lame. Nobody is perfect, and I implore you to answer honestly.

1. The spring dance is literally right around the corner. Your friends have dates, the limo has been paid for, and the saucy black number you plan on wearing is available in your size at your favorite boutique. Unfortunately, you don't have a date yet. There are a few good date options left, but you're unsure if any of the available cuties are planning on asking you so last minute. You:

   a. Decide you don't want to go to the dance without a date but you also don't want to ask a guy. It isn't Sadie Hawkins, after all. You wait it out and determine that if nobody asks you by the day of, you'll stay home.

   b. Wear your best outfit to school and muster up the courage to ask one of the guys to be your date.

   c. Make plans out of town. You're pretty sure no one is going to ask you.

   d. Go by yourself to the dance with your group of friends. It's more fun when you don't have to stick to one person all night anyway.

2. You text a guy you've been flirting with to see what he's up to that night, hoping that you'll get together.

He answers with a text that could be interpreted either way. It says, "No plans yet. You?" You decide to respond like this:

    a. "Me neither."

    b. "I'm getting hungry . . . for you!"

    c. "I'm getting hungry."

    d. "Thinking about dinner plans. Want to grab a bite?"

3. College applications are due this year. This is how you are handling the situation:

    a. You have your top three schools already picked out. You know you're totally getting in, so you will only apply to those three.

    b. You aren't sure where you want to go to school yet. Staying in state sounds pretty comfortable and reasonably priced. But the lure of going across the country is also strong. You'll apply to a mix of different universities and see where you get accepted.

    c. You're an athlete being recruited to play at two different schools. Both are out of state, and you'd be happy to attend either. They'll provide a totally new experience but the comfort of being close with your new teammates.

d. Your parents are pushing you to apply to their alma mater. You decide to go for it, even though you aren't sure if it's what you really want to do.

4. It's a hot Saturday afternoon, so you and your friends decide to hit the mall for some air-conditioning, shopping, and boy watching (like people watching, but focusing on boys only . . . clearly). In Forever 21, you try on an amazing shift dress and you come out of the dressing room to show your friends. Amy gives you her standard "meh" face, and Natalie thinks it's just okay. Your response:

   a. You check out your fine self in the mirror once again, looking for flaws but seeing only a stunning new look. You decide to purchase the dress anyway.

   b. You really value their opinions, so you ask them why they are lukewarm on it. Amy dislikes the color, and Natalie doesn't think her body type would work in the dress. You buy the dress, since now you understand why they aren't wild about it.

   c. Your smile quickly turns to a frown and you lie, saying that you really don't like it either.

   d. You want your friends to like the dress as much

as you do. You carry it around for a few minutes after trying it on but decide not to buy it.

5. You get along really well with your lab partner, who also happens to be one of the most popular guys at school. You're pleasantly surprised when he asks you out on a date, but you're afraid you don't really fit into the girly-girl mold. At school the day of the date, you:

    a. Wear a skirt and style your hair a little fancier than normal. No harm in looking nice, right?

    b. Come as his ex-girlfriend's doppelgänger. She always wore her hair straight, so you do too. She always eats a lollipop during morning break, so you whip one out during lab.

    c. Decide you aren't as into him as you thought. Turns out you like the idea of dating him, but you're not interested in a real relationship. You go on the date anyway, though, because canceling would be rude (and ruin things if you changed your mind again).

    d. Act and dress just like you do any other day. You don't mention the date during lab because that would be . . . awkward.

6. It's your first year at college, and you and Bobby have been dating a few months. Thanksgiving is coming up,

and because his family lives far away, you make plans to spend the holiday together with your family. Your parents and Bobby haven't met. What happens? You:

a. Force your parents to keep your nerdy ninth-grade band photos hidden away. The glasses phase in your life was four years ago, and the pics should remain hidden in their current, undisclosed location.

b. Let Bobby know—before you head off to eat turkey—that your parents said they'd be more comfortable if Bobby sleeps on the couch rather than shacking up with you, and you begrudgingly agreed.

c. E-mail your parents a strict list of no-no topics of conversation. You also e-mail Bobby a list of things to avoid.

d. Get really angry with Bobby, who went out with his friends the night before the trip and had a little too much fun instead of getting ready to leave, and you decide to leave without him.

7. Ever since your sixth-grade field trip to the observatory, you've loved to look at the cosmos. A little science-nerdy, sure, but unique nonetheless. Your love affair with space is so serious that, for your birthday, your parents bought you the high-powered telescope you'd

been dreaming of. Before your crush comes to your house for the first time, you:

   a. Hide your telescope and manuals in your brother's closet and make no mention of your weekly Sunday-night outings to the observatory.

   b. Decide to let your crush know about your obsession only if you hit the six-month relationship mark.

   c. Leave your telescope out in plain view. You're a little nervous as to what he might say, but you're praying he'll think it's interesting.

   d. Suggest the observatory as a first date. You'll be sure to impress him with your knowledge of the heavens.

8. School is finally out, and you have ninety days of summer ahead. Those ninety days look something like this:

   a. You take on a serious internship at a software company. You'll work five days a week, but the payoff will be résumé bliss.

   b. You suggest to your friends that you all help out at your local animal shelter a few days a week. You won't get totally off track, and you'll be spending time with animals, something you find rewarding.

c. You pick up applications for a few different jobs because a paycheck sounds absolutely awesome. When the time comes to actually turn in the apps, though, you decide that the idea of long days simmering on the beach appeals to you more.

d. You really want to take a cooking class that meets two days a week. Your mom, on the other hand, forces you to get a job, telling you that work experience will serve you better.

9. It's Saturday night. Your best friend is having a blow-out party. You haven't even started to write your five-page art history paper due at nine Monday morning. Your brilliant self decides to:

a. Go to the party, obviously.

b. Go to the party, but create an outline for the paper beforehand. Sure, you'll arrive an hour late, but getting some work done makes you feel more confident in your ability to get the paper done on time.

c. Go to the party, but promise yourself that you'll be in bed by midnight and up by eight a.m. on Sunday to get working. As it always turns out, this doesn't end up happening. You're home at two a.m. and up at noon.

d.   You decide to miss the party in order to write.
      You're so motivated that the work is done by
      eleven on Saturday night. Turns out that you
      write so fast, a little socializing may not have
      hurt after all.

THE RESULTS

Tally up your points based on the results below. My personal
answers are in boldface. Afterward, we'll discuss what your
score means.

1.   a-1, b-3, c-4, **d-2**
2.   a-2, b-4, c-1, **d-3**
3.   a-4, **b-2**, c-3, d-1
4.   a-4, b-3, c-1, **d-2**
5.   **a-3**, b-1, c-2, d-4
6.   a-2, **b-3**, c-4, d-1
7.   a-1, b-2, **c-3**, d-4
8.   a-4, b-3, **c-2**, d-1
9.   a-1, **b-3**, c-2, d-4

*I scored 23 points!

WHAT YOUR SCORE MEANS
9–15 POINTS: BABY STEPS

You haven't yet quite figured out where you are headed in life.
And that's not a bad thing, sweetheart. Far too often, girls think
they have to have everything: college choice, major, career, mar-

riage age, and so forth picked out before they even leave the womb! It's just not so, because the more you explore who you are through a multitude of experiences, the better off you'll be. What if you've always planned on being a doctor, but when you find yourself in med school you *hate* it? The trick is to stick to your guns and act on those small inklings of interest. Who cares if your friends think debate team is lame? You may go on to be a corporate lawyer and laugh all the way to the bank.

16–22 Points: Feeling a Bit Wishy-Washy?

That's because you are, dear friend. You think your mind is made up, only to switch positions after making a commitment. First you want to learn ballet, then you want to be a law student, then you decide that NASA may be your thing. Your inability to decide also extends itself to your relationships with guys. Do you want a boyfriend? Maybe you do. Maybe you don't. Maybe you do. At the very least, you are figuring out the things you don't like and don't want to do on your quest for awesomeness. Try sticking with something a little longer, though. It may end up surprising you.

23–30 Points: Oozing Confidence

Okay, we get it. You know what you like and who you are or want to become, and you are proud of it! You're already a follower of the Golden Rule, even if you didn't know it until now. You've already made some mistakes and are bound to make some more, but you have a clear sense of what to avoid from here on out. Whether it's boys, jobs, or lipstick, you know what you want at this very moment. Your future is bright, even though you aren't sure if what's going on now will last forever. You're so happy with yourself, however, that you sure hope it does.

31–36 POINTS: STUCK IN YOUR WAYS

Wanted to go to Harvard since you were five? Know that you'll get married when you're twenty-seven? Finished that paper early because you couldn't bear to drag it out any longer? I'm sure some of this sounds at least remotely familiar. Loosen up before your head implodes (and that would be a shame, because you are so pretty). Life is never, ever, ever going to go exactly as planned, and the sooner you understand that, the less let down you'll feel if your dreams fall apart. Maybe Harvard won't accept you. Take your dear author for example. My alma mater, UCLA, didn't accept me right out of high school. I had a backup plan, though: dominate at UCSB for two years, then transfer. And I did! So, do *you* have a backup plan you're comfortable with too? I love that you have your head on straight, but becoming too set in your premeditated ways is actually riskier than you realize (and are probably comfortable with). Why so? The setback of having everything you were counting on fall apart sucks pretty bad. Life happens, you know? Create that backup plan now!

TYPES OF GIRLS

As we continue to focus on you and only you, I hope you have a clear understanding of my reasoning behind categorizing girls into different types based on desires, maturity levels, passions, and ideas. The types I will describe fit into the different categories the previous quiz revealed. I'm doing it to show you from an outsider's point of view how relationships are affected by where you are in life, not to hurt your feelings or point out flaws.

Different maturity levels allow for different kinds of relationships with guys. To me, maturity is based on self-awareness, which relates directly to life experience. If you're a young person, it's likely that you don't have a whole lot of life experience yet. If you don't yet know who you are or where you want to be, how can you be expected to know what kind of relationship is right for you? You don't, but that's where I'm stepping in to make your life easier. I absolutely want you to indulge in your own self-discovery, but I also want you to intelligently skip the bad relationship experiences that come along with not quite knowing who you are.

So, how will you skip all the nasty stuff while still having meaningful relationships? First, by remembering the warning signs for icky guys you've just learned. Second, and more important, by believing in yourself. It's a crucial stepping-stone to figuring out who you are, anyway, so it's beneficial to take it on as your mantra this very second.

Look at it this way: Believing in who you are on your own terms is the mantra and Golden Rule of this book, my life, and the lives of every successful person you can think of. There simply isn't enough time in the day for self-doubt, because all it does is drag you down. It shuts off your moral compass and leads you straight to heartache and trouble. Remember Rachel and Marco? His disappearing act led her to believe he didn't want anything serious from her, which in turn made her doubt her value as a lovable person. She felt like she wasn't worthy of a relationship, simply because Marco didn't want one. In retrospect, had Rachel followed the Golden Rule, she would have avoided all that messy, upside-down nonsense. She needed to believe in herself, but just because she didn't then doesn't mean she won't in the future.

So! Take the categories and their corresponding types I'm about to discuss with a grain of salt. If you're not happy with your spot, acknowledge that your disdain for it is a good thing. We've all been there. I was a Wishy-Washy type for years, and I'm not afraid to tell you that all it got me into was trouble. My day of enlightenment came when a new friend and I were talking about boys (of course). She was shocked to discover that none of the boys I dated for fun ever materialized into a full-blown relationship. When she said that to me, instead of feeling carefree and cool about it (which is how I used to feel), I experienced a tinge of embarrassment. Let's just say that when you feel embarrassed about your actions, you're officially ready to move on from them.

So, let's be awkward and cringe about our mishaps (few and far between, of course) together just long enough to acknowledge that it's time to put them to rest. Your categorization is simply a reflection of the girl you're leaving behind today—you'll be avoiding future messes with my help and consideration.

Your goal at the end of this journey is to find yourself moving from your current category into the Oozing Confidence zone and subsequent types. It is here that you will find the best relationships with others, because you find yourself living by the Golden Rule. You love yourself, and others will love you too.

THE JUGGLER

The Juggler, like so many of us, loves, loves, loves, loves, loves boys. Everything about them makes her swoon: their soft hair, the way they say her name while staring into her eyes, the way they pull her in for hugs. The right guy for her would fill all her relationship dreams: They would fall madly in love, never argue, and enjoy all the same things.

To her, that is the perfect relationship. And it's not surprising that she believes in this ideal: fairy tales, movies, and stories have taught her about this particular kind of romance from a very young age.

Her issue is that she doesn't yet have enough serious relationship experience to understand that a boyfriend comes with guaranteed ups and downs, and that one or two minor disputes is not enough to end things forever. She juggles boys because she hopes one will rise above the rest to be her Prince Charming.

If her crush from geometry class doesn't return her text, she'll give attention to the cute boy on the basketball team instead. If Max doesn't call, she'll send Eric a flirty Facebook message. She is looking for positive attention, and if she doesn't get it when expected, she simply goes to another source to reaffirm her belief in the power of love.

Boys, however, do not appreciate being juggled, just as girls find it to be inconsiderate. The Juggler will eventually slip up and drop the ball. When one falls, all the others are bound to come crashing down around her as well.

In order for the Juggler to stop the circus act and have that fairy-tale romance, she needs to pick the guy she likes best and go for it. Only then will she learn that small issues can be worked through and won't ruin her perfect relationship in the making.

BOYFRIEND? WHAT BOYFRIEND?

Have you ever met the kind of girl who sometimes denies being in a relationship? These girls are few and far between, but they definitely exist. Now, why would a girl deny that she has a boyfriend? First let's talk about who she is denying this to, and then we'll discuss why she is doing it.

Maybe Denial Danielle is not being truthful with her parents about having a boyfriend. For whatever reason, it's a little uncomfortable for some to bring up a new boyfriend to a parent. This frequently stems from some embarrassment regarding growing up. Here's some good advice: Just tell them. Your world won't end. In fact, your parents will most likely appreciate your honesty (and be superexcited for you). They'll probably want to meet this young man, and you should let them. They have seen a lot more than you have and will be far more comfortable with you growing up if you're honest with them from the start.

Second, if Denial Danielle is denying her relationship to

her friends, she is wading in water that's a little too deep. The rationale behind denying her boyfriend's existence to her friends is that she is embarrassed about liking him for one reason or another. Perhaps he isn't the coolest guy in school or he dresses a little funny. If Danielle can't be honest about who she likes, she is absolutely not worth her (probably) sweet boyfriend's time. She should stand up for the boys she likes, despite what others think about them. If she doesn't, she is just as bad as those who tease him.

Finally, if Danielle is denying that she has a boyfriend to other guys, she should be ready for some serious heartache. She is most likely pretending her guy isn't *her guy* in an attempt to trade up. What does this say about her? Nothing good. How would you feel if a guy did this to you, your sister, or one of your friends?

It's about respect, Danielle. Respect the people you love enough to be honest with others about them. In return, you'll find that people will respect *you* a lot more.

THE CHEATER

The Cheater is weak. She is insecure and responds to this personal issue through her indiscretions. When she cheats, she feels desired. She needs to feel desired in order to feel better about herself, and so she continues to do it.

The Cheaters need to look within themselves to discover what it is that makes them insecure. It is only after they isolate this issue and deal with it that they will stop hurting the people they love.

No one deserves to be treated with disrespect, especially by someone who is quick to give in to selfish desires driven by self-doubt. If you are a Cheater, do everyone a favor and remain single until you can figure out what causes you to treat yourself and the people you care about badly.

GIRLS WHO ARE WISHY-WASHY
First Sign of Trouble

In high school I was a First Sign of Trouble girl. This is a girl, like the Juggler, who has an ideal image of what a relationship with a guy should be. I wanted a boyfriend whose personality flowed easily alongside my own, who didn't turn me off in any way, and who never forgot to call or text me about my Friday-night plans.

Unlike the Juggler, though, an FSOT girl doesn't continually go back to guys who occasionally do what isn't desired of them. FSOT girls immediately move on when they notice even minor details about a guy that they don't like—that's what I did.

Maybe he wears funny shoes. Maybe his thin mustachio grows in a little too ginger for your taste. Perhaps his laugh is slightly high pitched. To quote Liz Lemon, "That's a deal-breaker, ladies." Also important to note, Liz Lemon is chronically single, as are all First Sign of Trouble girls.

FSOT girls do want relationships, though. She gets that relationships are sometimes a give and take. She just doesn't want to give in on the things that bug her from the start.

In order for any FSOT girl to move into the Oozing Confidence category, she has to ditch the overly judgmental attitude. Just as you want a guy to love you for you, the First Sign of Trouble girl needs to learn to love a guy for who he is as well. In the long run, looks fade, but personality lasts forever. I've learned to let the little things go and focus on what's more important: people's good qualities.

THE FLIRT

In addition to being a First Sign of Trouble girl, I was also the Flirt. Who is this girl, and what does she do?

Clearly, flirting up a storm is part of her romantic and even platonic relationships. She teases boys, gives them sly glances, and pokes fun at their hairdos. She has excellent people skills and is not shy about utilizing them to her advantage. Maybe she truly likes her flirting partner of the moment, maybe she doesn't. It really doesn't matter to the Flirt. She's doing it just for the way it makes her feel: fun, desired, and confident.

The Flirt, despite her mood-enhancing loquaciousness, doesn't tend to have a wandering eye. She is able to find her match and lock it down, but it's her inability to keep her mouth closed that starts to bother her mate. She is definitely not a cheater—she would never go that far. She simply likes to have a little fun, but it wears on her boyfriends because they feel like they may not be the *only* one for her.

For the Flirt to be considered serious GF material, she has to learn to keep her teasing under wraps. A serious show of commitment is often required for the Flirt's guy to understand that despite her vivacious personality, she really is a one-guy kind of girl. As silly as it seems, in this day and age some serious deleting of cell phone contacts and Facebook friends may be in order.

ONE OF THE GUYS

There are always girls who are good friends with all the guys. In fact, they probably get along better with boys than they do with girls. Maybe they have brothers instead of sisters and they've been dealing with dudes since they were in the cradle.

There is also a strong likelihood that a girl who is just "one of the guys" has a serious thing for one or two of them. Truth be told, most likely the guy has no idea, as they've been friends for years and nothing more. She treats all the guys the same— as buddies—instead of actually making her feelings known.

This type of girl is hesitant to make a move because she worries that her friendships with these people may be strained if the feelings aren't reciprocated. She sees how other girls, like the Flirt, act around her boys, and she finds it to be pure entertainment. She isn't a girly girl, but those feelings for a guy still exist. She wonders how she can go from being one of the guys to being girlfriend material without making a total fool of herself.

How does she do it? Through honesty. As scary as it is, making feelings known to a friend frequently results in the reciprocation of those feelings. If you like someone and have a great relationship, chances are they like you back. It's sometimes worth taking a leap of faith to see if what you think is there really does exist. Only by taking that risk will the girl who is one of the guys, turn into the girlfriend of one of the guys.

GIRLS WHO OOZE CONFIDENCE
THE LONG-TERM GIRLFRIEND

The Long-Term Girlfriend is a long-term girlfriend for a reason. She has figured out how to make her relationship work with her sweetie. How does she do this?

First, she is honest with herself about who she is. Second, she is honest with her boyfriend about who she is. A note about honesty, though: This kind of honesty, about oneself and those you love, isn't something that comes easily. People work their entire lives to reach this level of self-awareness. The Long-Term Girlfriend's relationship with her integrity is a work in progress, as is the case with any young person, but she understands the importance of honesty in a relationship on a fundamental level.

Third, both people in the relationship have learned how to

make small changes for their partner without changing who they are. The Long-Term Girlfriend has learned to focus on the big picture and knows that these sorts of concessions can help a relationship. For example, she loves to text message her friends at all hours of the day, but it really bothered her boyfriend that she wasn't able to focus on him more while they *were* together. She thought his request to cut out the texting around him was pesky, but she agreed to talk to her friends on her own time. Had she not done this, her boyfriend's annoyance would have slowly changed from frustration with the situation to frustration with her. It would probably have led to a fight, and then another, and potentially the end of their relationship. And over text messages? That's pretty childish.

Yes, the Long-Term Girlfriend sees the advantages of making small changes in order to keep the peace. But her boyfriend appreciates this and does the same for her, because it's certain that there are small things about him that are sometimes bothersome. Take Rob and Maria, for example. They work together, and they are also in a committed relationship. Erica is the office flirt and spends a hefty amount of time e-mailing Rob while shooting death rays from her eyeballs at Maria. Rob interprets Erica's friendliness as friendship, but the flirting makes Maria very uncomfortable.

Maria knows that Rob considers Erica a fun work friend, but Maria asks him to spend a little less time around her every day. When she asks him to do this, she makes sure to explain to him clearly why she feels uncomfortable with Erica. She understands that she cannot make demands of her boyfriend without being honest about her request. It was only because she spoke up that Rob realized how uncomfy it made his girlfriend, and because Erica's friendship isn't exactly paramount to him, he happily gives in to her wishes.

Overall, the Long-Term Girlfriend realizes that a relationship is give and take, and by subscribing to this reality, she encounters less opportunity to feel resentful of her partner. In the case that either person in the relationship makes a request that goes too far, they discuss both sides of the issue so that each is fully aware of where the other stands.

Whether a person is asking too much of his or her partner is based on particular, personal issues. How I feel about an issue may be interpreted differently by the Long-Term Girlfriend and her guy. She takes each situation as it comes, and if her guy can't agree to the initial request, then the Long-Term Girlfriend and her man compromise on the compromise, until they've both reached an agreement that is satisfying.

JUMPING JENNY

We all know a Jumping Jenny: the girl who meets a guy and jumps right into a relationship with him. As crazy as it seems, Jumping Jenny may be on to something the rest of us aren't.

She has enough negative experiences under her belt with guys from her past to know that when a nice guy comes along who connects with her immediately, and values her true self, including her quirks and her weird family, he is worth holding on to. The mysterious emotion behind this immediate connection? True love. Despite what any scrooge will tell you, it really does exist. That's why when it takes hold of Jumping Jenny, she pays attention. She knows that true love is hard to find, impossible to ignore, and wonderful beyond belief.

It takes a girl as confident in herself as Jumping Jenny is to allow herself to dive into what others perceive as being a little nutty. Only she knows how she feels, and she doesn't allow herself to be swayed by her friends' and family's insistence that she's moving too fast.

She understands, just like the Long-Term Girlfriend, that problems are guaranteed to arise and are fixable with compromise. More often than not, it's the little things that build up that tear couples apart. Jumping Jenny and her boyfriend stop hiccups immediately as they arise, through their honesty and devotion to each other.

The Breakup Girl

At first glance, the Breakup Girl seems to belong in the Wishy-Washy category. And she may, if she goes back and forth between wanting a relationship or not, which results in a breakup.

She absolutely belongs in the Oozing Confidence category, however, if she breaks up with guys because she feels that the proper connection between them just isn't there.

The Breakup Girl is the type I'd like to see more young women subscribe to. Not because I want to see them go through a lot of breakups (which are unavoidably depressing) but because they have reached a level of self-awareness that allows them to understand that a failed relationship is not the end of the world but instead a rebirth. A failed partnership is an opportunity to create a better one. Her self-assurance reminds her that a breakup is not a reflection of her worth but rather a funny-shaped puzzle piece that simply doesn't match up to her own.

She doesn't stay in a floundering relationship, because she knows that more successful ones lie in her future. In order to move forward, though, she understands that a breakup is a part of it.

The Breakup Girl has definitely been broken up with before, but it's because of this that she is quick to pull the plug if it isn't working out with Mr. Not Prince Charming. She has learned that it is easier and kinder to do the deed sooner rather than later, empathizing with her soon-to-be ex instead of holding him responsible.

GIRLS WHO ARE STUCK IN THEIR WAYS
Gives It Up Girl

Gives It Up Girl is every best friend's worst nightmare. She snags a great guy and virtually disappears off the face of the planet. Forget Friday night with GIU Girl: she already has plans with her beloved. Never mind that you called her Tuesday and she hasn't gotten back to you; she was just superbusy . . . with her boyfriend.

I'm not sure why girls sometimes give so much of themselves to their romantic relationship that their platonic relationships suffer. Perhaps they're afraid of losing their guy, or perhaps they sincerely enjoy spending time with their guy over others in their life. If a Gives It Up Girl truly enjoys her boyfriend, good for her, but what about all the other people who care about her? All relationships are give and take, and if she gives only to her boyfriend she is taking away quite a bit from her friends as a result.

And the reality of giving everything up for the guy she loves so much? When eventually the spark fades, the friends she ditched won't be there anymore to help pick up the pieces.

In addition, if a girl lovingly gives it all up for her boyfriend, he is bound to become used to this behavior. Down the line if she realizes her error, chances are he won't respond positively to her desire to get out, see her friends and do whatever she wants at the drop of a hat. He'll likely be confused and want the relationship to return to the way it's always been.

A little advice for a GIU Girl: Take it slow. When you meet a guy, remember that he is still just a guy and that your friends and family should rank a lot higher than he does in importance. Realize that guys love freedom in a relationship, so stop worrying that if you give it to him, you'll lose him as a result. The exact opposite is true: If you let your guy do his thing, he'll be thankful that you allow him to be himself. He will come home every night more committed to you than ever. And until you know him well enough to make a serious commitment, keep seeing your friends, too. Plan girls' nights and send out group e-mails to keep everyone in the loop. Small signs of goodwill will go a long way in keeping all your relationships, both romantic and platonic, intact.

Noncommitment Girl

Noncommitment Girl's reason for never having a boyfriend? She is simply too busy with all her résumé-enhancing commitments, obviously. Come on, sweetie. Absolutely no person on earth is so busy they can't make room for love in their life.

Interestingly enough, a little lovin' would probably make all the things she is working so hard to accomplish that much easier. A great relationship doesn't burden her or her time or limit what she wants to do in life. A great relationship supports everything she is about and all the amazing stuff she wants to accomplish.

The longer she forces herself to avoid relationships (because that's what she's doing), the more hardened she will become. She will get to the point where having a relationship becomes something that is scary and ominous, because she believes that by giving in to one she will lose everything else she is working on. Yes, it's a control issue, friends, and because relationships are unpredictable she feels like if she has one, the rest of her carefully calibrated, foolproof routine will go out the window.

In addition, the later she allows herself to finally start having relationships, the longer it will be before she learns what kind of relationship is right for her. Because she won't yet have experienced all the stuff that younger girls have gone through, she'll date guys she considers to be age appropriate only to find that they have already successfully dealt with all the relationship issues she is just now learning about.

It's easy for Noncommitment Girl to let her life be solely about her. She has to realize, though, that her life is about more than just herself—it's also about her family, her friends, and one day, maybe even a husband and family of her own. The sooner she is able to welcome something wonderfully fulfilling into her life besides school and work, the more well-rounded, and well-adjusted she'll be.

GOIN' TO THE CHAPEL GIRL

Calm down, girl. Not every guy you date is your future hubby. In fact, encountering or becoming this girl is most likely a few years off. But sure, write out your first name in front of his last name. Browse the Tiffany website for your perfect engagement ring. Pick out colors for your wedding party. But don't treat every guy you meet as if he is yours till death do you part!

Why? Well, first, because this sort of seriousness is bound to scare a few dudes off. Guys like to get serious with the right girl over a period of time—not five seconds into dating. Push your hopes and dreams of becoming Mrs. So-and-So onto your perfect new boyfriend right away and you'll probably end up eating ice cream alone on Saturday night.

In addition, a Goin' to the Chapel Girl tends to clutch on to the idea of getting married so tightly, that she is blinded by real signals that her current relationship is faltering. She ignores the issue rather than dealing with it, under the misconception that the appearance of a perfect relationship is what will walk her down the aisle. Perhaps she is being treated badly, but because they've discussed marriage she sticks it out. Perhaps he isn't the right guy for her, but because they've been together for three years, she keeps moving forward.

Whatever the case is, Goin' to the Chapel Girl needs to understand that there is a perfect guy for her out there. He may not be the first guy she meets or the guy she has dated the longest. The nervous feelings she gets sometimes from her relationship should be addressed rather than swept under the rug. Only when she is true to herself will she be able to act in a responsible way on issues that come up, and in a way that doesn't allow her to disregard herself.

LOVE LIST

Enough typecasting for a few pages. You know the overall category you fit into and were probably able to pick out a subtype or two for yourself. In high school I was a Wishy-Washy Flirt. How about you?

Chances are, you're unsatisfied with what I wrote and not happy with yourself for falling into category x, y, or z. "Unsatisfied" is exactly the reaction I was hoping to draw from you. Unfortunately, sometimes it takes another person (me, again) pointing out what you're missing in order for you to make some positive changes. And now that I've done that and you're a little uncomfortable, we can work together to bring out the best version of you.

Think of me as your relationship coach. First I had to teach you all about the sucky stuff in order to enlighten you about its unfortunate existence. Then I taught you why the Golden Rule will allow you to move past the yucky stuff without getting too deep into it yourself. And now I get to teach you *how* to follow the rule through a strong self-awareness.

We've been chatting for about ninety pages now about why believing in yourself will lead you to successful relationships. I'm sure you're sick of it. But how, exactly, does a person do that, believe in themselves, apart from simply keeping it in mind? They take carefully crafted steps to remind them of all the special reasons why they love themselves. Once these qualities are identified, it's easy to find comfort in them, leading to a greater overall belief in oneself.

The steps, exercises—whatever you want to call them—are rather fun and are guaranteed to generate a warm, fuzzy feeling inside you. That's the whole point, really—to feel good about who you are. The first exercise we'll do is create your personal Love List, where you write down what you absolutely adore about yourself.

In order to begin the Love List, let go of all the nastiness we've encountered so far. It's time to become totally, completely self-indulgent. To prepare yourself, maybe you should park yourself in the loveliest part of your home, throw on some jewelry and lip gloss, and mix up a delicious juice beverage, complete with straw and little umbrella.

The Love List, and its accompanying behavior, may seem

silly. Don't take it for granted, though, dears. It will show you why you're already amazing and why believing in yourself will turn you into an even more accomplished person. As an added bonus, this exceptionally fabulous version of you will draw the boyfriend of your dreams in that much closer. And why will it bring that amazing guy closer to you? Because guys respect girls who respect themselves, who have their own ideas about what is cool, and who have their own lives. The guy you're crushing on big-time probably thinks it's cool that you hit up the observatory with your dad every Thursday or that you walk dogs at your local animal shelter on the weekends. Stop hiding it!

THE EXERCISE

It's pretty simple, really. Take out a sheet of paper or just use the blank form you'll find on the page after *my* personal list. The list you'll create consists of the twenty things you love the most about yourself. Your list is totally personal, so put down anything and everything. Go beyond twenty. I mean it. And then post it in a spot you will see it every day. If you're too embarrassed to do that (out of fear that someone—say, your brother—will see it), keep it in this book and refer to it whenever you're feeling a little blue. This list will not only cheer you up, it will help you become the kind of girl who utilizes the Golden Rule for herself every day. This girl knows that if it doesn't work out with him, *he is just not the right guy for her*, NOT the misconception that "I must not be right for him."

Lo's Love List

I love myself because . . .

1. I can make homemade bread.
2. Writing is one of my favorite hobbies.
3. I can spread my toes so wide, they look like aliens.
4. I'm not afraid to swim in the ocean.
5. I go to the movies by myself.
6. I like to hike with my dad at seven in the morning when I'm at my parents' house.
7. I can sometimes cream the old dudes playing bocce on the beach.
8. I can make my brother smile.
9. I look out for my friends.
10. I am a bad liar, so I always tell the truth.
11. I graduated from UCLA.
12. I love a lot of other people too.
13. I decorated my room by myself.
14. I rescued Chloe and Ollie from animal shelters.
15. I know who my true friends are.
16. I'm really good at arranging flowers.
17. I am a Kappa Kappa Gamma.
18. I love researching new cars.
19. I watch a lot of TV.
20. Other people love me too.

See? It's quite self-indulgent. But my list makes me feel good about myself, and yours should do the same for you. So have at it! I'm giving you thirty spaces, because I know you can come up with that many reasons why you love yourself. Don't complain that I'm wasting precious space in this book either. I'm the author—I can add as many pages as I want!

I love myself because . . .

1.

2.

3.

4.

5.

6.

7.

8.

9.

10.

11.

12.

13.

14.

15.

16.

17.

18.

19.

20.

21.

22.

23.

24.

25.

26.

27.

28.

29.

30.

MORE EXERCISES

In addition to the Love List, there are three other exercises you can do to help you reach an emotional level where believing in yourself isn't an option—it's a way of life. You will be thankful for what you have and who you are and come to understand that external forces rather than personal weakness are what cause problems.

SET GOALS

At first, the exercise of setting goals and reaching them may not seem to relate to having a great relationship. Getting the A+ you wanted on your math test certainly doesn't guarantee your math tutor will like you back. And yet . . . when you see something through, it shows you just what you're capable of doing, and that is a confidence booster. And confidence leads to relationships. *That's* how setting goals and having rocking boyfriends go hand in hand.

In addition, when you set goals, you are in control—in control of the goals and in control of yourself. By following the steps you lay out for yourself, occasional setbacks are a result of an external circumstance, not personal weakness. Also remember that when you accomplish your goal, you should celebrate! By recognizing your achievements, your confidence will build.

For starters, let's set three different types of goals for ourselves. Set yourself up for success by choosing goals that are realistic for you. Don't pick working for NASA if you're terrible with numbers. It just isn't gonna happen.

The first goal should be an immediate one, something you can accomplish within one week. The next goal should be long term, something you can accomplish within one year. The third goal should be exploratory. This is the goal that allows you to have a little fun, to try out whatever it is that you've been itching to do. In order to get you on the right track, I'll discuss some of my personal goals with you and give you some ideas in case you get stuck.

Immediate Goals
Time frame: Seven days
Goal: Exercise at spin class three times this week

I picked this goal for myself because after I spin, I feel energized, happy, and full of life. In addition to the obvious health benefits, this is the main reason that I like to exercise. I know that my body has a purpose! Its purpose is to make me feel good!

I always feel proud of myself after a spin class too. It's an hour of grueling, butt-kicking, drench-you-in-sweat hard work. I'm not an athlete, but I sure feel like one afterward. I love watching my progress from week to week. The bike's monitor shows how much work you're doing and at what intensity, and seeing it consistently go up is reason alone to keep going back. It's gratifying to know I'm working at something that keeps me healthy and motivated.

I chose my goal of three classes in seven days because I have a busy schedule and my goal helps to keep me on track. Sometimes I come home from work just wanting to watch television. By having a goal, though, I'm driven to do the exercise instead of turning on the TV. Accomplishing my goal creates a greater feeling of personal satisfaction than I would get from a ho-hum night of watching TV.

What kind of immediate goal should you set for yourself? Do you want to participate in an activity more often, like I do? If so, choose a part of your routine that makes you feel good. For example, if you rock art class, maybe you want to enroll in drawing at the local art center. Perhaps your activity, and by no means does it have to be drawing (I draw stick figures), reinforces something on your Love List. By choosing something that allows you some fun *and* reinforces your awesomeness, the satisfaction you receive will be a double whammy of self-efficiency and self-love.

Do you want to incorporate something new into your weekly routine? If so, set a reasonable immediate goal. For example, if you want to read a new book every week, choose one that isn't too long and with a subject that interests you. Set yourself up for success rather than failure. You are in control of the setting of the goals, the execution of them, and their completion as well. Choose wisely, and remind yourself just how efficient you can be. It's a great feeling.

LONG-TERM GOALS
TIME FRAME: SIX MONTHS TO ONE YEAR
GOAL: WRITE A CHILDREN'S BOOK IN THE NEXT TWELVE MONTHS

I think it's clear to you as a reader that I love to write. One of the primary reasons I began to write creatively is the work I do with a children's literacy organization. I read books to underprivileged preschool-aged children to help them reach a kindergarten reading level by the time they enter elementary school. I love spending time with these kids. Their faces light up when you read to them, and they're entranced by the storytelling and the flow of the words.

Participating in this organization inspires me to continue helping out in my community through reading, but it has also sparked my interest in writing a children's book myself. I believe in my creativity enough that I know I could create a spirited story for these kids. If I were able to publish the story, it would create a permanent addition to the library of children's literature. Even on days when I couldn't be in their class in person, I would be there on the shelf in spirit.

My long-term goal is a lofty one, but that doesn't mean you shouldn't set the bar just as high for yourself. By making it a long-term goal, you allow yourself the time needed to accomplish something great. And it's okay if your goal is a mix of personal and professional. Frequently, achieving a professional or educational goal results in great personal happiness.

For example, my goal is important for me professionally because it would represent my expansion as an author into multiple genres. On a personal note, it would mean the world to me, as it relates to the children I teach. On an even more personal note, I would love to write a children's book to see the look on my own (future) children's faces when they realize that what they're reading was written by their mom.

That last part was a little silly to admit, but it would be special for me. So pick a goal that would hold real significance for you, too. When you accomplish it, you'll be astonished by how much you can get done when you're confident in your abilities.

Exploratory Goals

Time frame: Chosen based on objective

Goal: Complete a twelve-week culinary course

I absolutely love to cook, but a secret dream of mine has always been to take it to the next level. I'm not talking executive-chef-at-a-four-star-restaurant level, but at least good enough to serve Christmas dinner to the whole family (about thirty of us). Perhaps I'm the next Giada and I won't know it until I try.

I've always been nervous about jumping into something like this for a few reasons. First reason: culinary courses are very expensive, and I worry that I wouldn't be able to complete it for some scheduling reason and that the money would go to waste. My second concern is that people will think I'm crazy for taking culinary courses despite having little interest in ever working at a restaurant.

That's what an exploratory goal is for. To tell your critics, especially yourself, to shut up and just do it. No one can make you feel silly unless you treat your goal that way too. And there is a reason you have that innermost desire. You were born with it, and it will make you unique. Act on it now, when you're young and have time to figure out who or what you want to be. Maybe you'll end up hating whatever it is you try out. At least then you'll know for sure one way or the other, and you'll be thrilled that you decided to find out for yourself.

GIVE YOUR TIME AND ENERGY TO OTHERS

Philanthropy is a tool that not only helps others in important ways, but helps build the person you are as well. It's natural to feel good after you do good work for others. It's a positive cycle that will continue to better you as long as you're willing to participate.

When you are a successful volunteer, other people believe in the good in you. It feels nice to be believed in. It picks you up when you are down. It reminds you of how fortunate you are to be able to lend a hand to others.

In addition, when you give your time and energy to others, you'll get positive feedback in return. These are the building blocks for self-respect; when you know that others believe in you, it's easier to believe in yourself.

Giving your time and energy to others can be as simple as donating old clothes to your local shelter or as complicated as throwing a fund-raiser for clean drinking water. Simply adopting pets rather than buying them makes a positive impact larger than you can imagine. Whatever it is that you do, you are giving your time, so just choose the cause that feels right to you. The following list gives examples of organizations that would love to have you on their team:

Elizabeth Glaser Pediatric Aids Foundation

Phone: (888) 499-HOPE (4673)

Web: www.pedaids.org

E-mail: info@pedaids.org

American Humane Association

Phone: (800) 227-4645

Web: www.americanhumane.org

E-mail: info@americanhumane.org

Helen Keller International

Phone: (877) KELLER-4 (535-5374)

Web: www.hki.org

E-mail: info@hki.org

Susan G. Komen for the Cure

Phone: (877) GO KOMEN (465-6636)

Web: ww5.komen.org

Child Find of America

Phone: (800) I-AM-LOST

Web: www.childfindofamerica.org

Marine Toys for Tots Foundation

Web: www.toysfortots.org

RAINFOREST ALLIANCE

PHONE: (888) MY-EARTH

WEB: WWW.RAINFOREST-ALLIANCE.ORG

HABITAT FOR HUMANITY INTERNATIONAL

PHONE: (800) 422-4828

WEB: WWW.HABITAT.ORG

E-MAIL: IVP@HABITAT.ORG

AMERICAN RED CROSS

WEB: WWW.REDCROSS.ORG/EN/VOLUNTEERTIME

YMCA OF THE UNITED STATES

PHONE: (800) 872-9622

WEB: WWW.YMCA.NET

JUMPSTART

PHONE: (857) 413-4588

WEB: WWW.READFORTHERECORD.ORG

E-MAIL: RFTR@JSTART.ORG

IDENTIFY AN IDOL

Everyone has somebody they look up to, admire, and aspire to take after. Identifying an idol helps you to live vicariously through a person who inspires you. As you learn why they are successful and apply their methods to your own life, you start to identify their success with your own. It's a great way to build confidence in what you're doing. You know that what has worked for someone else can work for you, too, so it removes self-doubt from the equation.

So, what kind of qualities are you looking for in an idol? Choose a female idol for now, but feel free to have male idols in your life as well. You idol should:

- experience success because of dedication and hard work
- relate to your life in a personal way through common interests or dislikes
- exhibit integrity in her day-to-day life
- be respectful of others and their differences
- have the courage to stand up for the people and things that she believes in
- exhibit kindness and compassion toward others

One of my favorite female idols is Kelly Ripa. She is smart and sassy with a personality that lights up a room. I have never watched an episode of *Regis & Kelly* in which she was not a vivacious, understanding friend. You can tell that Kelly has a strong sense of self: she is comfortable being funny and self-deprecating, she enjoys talking about her family, and she has strong likes and dislikes.

Apart from her sparkly personality, I admire her career path and work ethic. She is a true success story: Making the switch from soaps to a talk show is not easy. She did it with grace and respect and was able to fill Kathie Lee's shoes by creating her own on-camera personality, one completely different from that of her predecessor.

In addition, I love that Kelly is a mom who seems completely comfortable in her role. She is simultaneously a TV host, mother, and wife. And she pulls it all off with flying colors.

Kelly Ripa is one of my idols because she is living a life that I admire and am building for myself. I'm so excited to take the next step into marriage, having a family, and rocking it at work. I want love, family, and career to be the building blocks in my life, and if Kelly can do it all, then so can I.

Pick someone who has created a life for herself that you admire, as I have done. It doesn't have to be a celebrity or a politician or successful businesswoman. You idol could be much closer to home: your mother, your sister, or a friend. Whoever she is, identify the reasons why she is a person to admire. If you incorporate these admirable aspects of her life into yours, you're bound to feel personal satisfaction.

To help get you started, here's a short list of women who would be great idols for any girl:

- Oprah Winfrey
- Michelle Obama

- Arianna Huffington
- Tina Fey
- Tyra Banks

Once you've chosen your idol, answer the following questions:

- What is it about this person that I admire?
- What qualities does she have that I hope to emulate?
- How did she become a success, and can I follow in my own life the steps she took?

PART 3

BELIEVING IN
THE RIGHT GUY

IMAGINE THAT YOU'RE BAKING A CAKE FOR YOUR BEST FRIEND'S birthday. First you read the directions. It's important to lay out some sort of game plan for all the different ingredients. Then you cream the sugar and butter together. In a separate bowl, you mix together all the dry ingredients. Add one egg at a time to the butter concoction you've got going. Finally, mix the dry ingredients together with the liquid ones. Throw it into a 350-degree oven for thirty minutes and voilà, you've created a cake!

Now consider all the time, energy, and dedication you put into creating your delectable masterpiece. It required you to select and read a recipe, learn how to put together all the components, and bake it for a while before you were rewarded with that tasty first bite.

Approaching romantic relationships is essentially the same, minus the messy ingredients all over your kitchen counter. As unromantic as it seems, creating the foundation for a delicious relationship requires a recipe. The recipe will instruct you regarding which ingredients are essential and at which point they should be added.

But, as with a cake, it's the quality and flavor of the ingredients and how they're combined that give the relationship its sweetness. Miss one crucial ingredient and your relationship, or your cake batter, is bound to fall apart in the oven.

I'm guessing that by now you're well enough acquainted with my analogies that instead of further explaining dessert essentials for three additional pages, I can move right into what I'm really getting at.

Just as a cake has a recipe, consider this guide to be your recipe, your outline, and your formula for successfully cooking up a fantastic relationship. Each chapter is an ingredient essential to the batter. Each chapter builds on the previous one, furthering the batter along before it's popped into the oven. Miss a chapter, skip a quiz, fast-forward a few pages, and you may miss an ingredient that is essential to what makes a good relationship really good.

I'm reflecting on this now because you have reached a point in the recipe where your batter is nearing completion. This part, Believing in the Right Guy, is the last ingredient you need before you start to bake your relationship into the scrumptious, delightful, amazing cakey goodness it can be. And any good pastry chef always does a final rundown of her recipe before she puts the batter into the oven.

Let's do that right now. So, we know this guide is the overall recipe to creating a completely thrilling relationship. The Golden Rule is the first step in the recipe. You have to follow the first step correctly or else the rest of the recipe is a disaster in the making. So, you let go of all the misconceptions, preconceptions, whatever-ceptions of what you mistakenly thought was the underlying rule of relationships and accept the Golden Rule. The Golden Rule teaches you that if it doesn't work out with a guy, it's not that you weren't right for him, it's that *he was not the right guy for you.* With this knowledge you undertake the second step.

The second step is to understand that the Baddies are the types of guys who make you feel like the opposite of the Golden Rule is true. You learn to point out the Baddies, understand why they are bad, and disregard them for guys who believe in you for who you already are.

Step three in the relationship recipe: Learn why believing in yourself is an essential ingredient. Believing in yourself brings the Golden Rule to life. Believing in yourself gives you the power to ignore the Baddies for guys who are worth your time. In addition, the third step teaches you *how* to believe in yourself if you need a gentle push in the right direction. It gives you empowering self-help tools that not only reinforce who you already are but turn that person into a girl others admire as well.

And now for step four: believing in the right guy. I know that so far I've taught you that a relationship is all about you. A lot of it is. You are one half of every relationship you have, and it's important to make sure that that half is well cared for and loved and feels good about herself.

Once you've reached this level of self-satisfaction, it's time to focus on the other half of what makes a relationship a relationship. Your boyfriend! You can do all the right things, but in order for a partnership to work, you need to get back what you put in. Your relationship will be successful only if this happens, so it's best to find a good guy who is committed to putting as much time and nurturing into growing your love as you do.

So, how do you find this guy? There are a few components involved. First, you have to let your guard down. This is hard to do, especially if you have been hurt before. It's a necessary step to take before you move forward, though. When you let your guard down, you put your faith in others. A relationship only works if that trust is there.

What will allow you to let your guard down is understanding that despite the occasional Baddie, most people are good people. Just like I've taught you signs that make the Baddies stick out like sore thumbs, I will teach you the signs that signal who these good guys are.

And what makes the good guys good? They respect others, treat them with kindness, and understand that every person is unique. They know that individualism is something to be regarded rather than scoffed at. They have a sense of right and wrong because they've experienced how hurtful "wrong" is and that "right" makes them feel a lot better. The good guys understand that it's essential to be compassionate to others in order to get the same respect back. The good guys are the ones who feel the same way about life as you do. You are for them what they are for you.

As boyfriends, the good guys are the ones who will let you be you, and love you for who that person is. They will encourage you to follow your dreams, make big plans, and live the life you've dreamed of, with them by your side.

They will expect the same support from you, though. This is an absolutely essential requirement of women in any relationship. If they believe in you, you must believe in them in return. They're the good guys, remember? They're worth it! They have hopes, dreams, and goals just like you do. Relationships are about mutual respect, and in terms of support, it's a mutual give and take between you. Be selfless and allow him to be who he really is. If you don't, you'll wind up as bad as one of the Baddies (but a girl, eww).

So, when you find a good guy for yourself—and trust me, they really do exist—celebrate your good fortune. Right off the bat you'll know that you're loved for being you and that he wouldn't have it any other way. The respect you've been trying to squeeze out of other lame guys for yourself is already in place. At the end of the day, that's what the good guys are all about. They love you for you because that girl is already good enough for them.

QUIZ: RECOGNIZING THE GOOD GUYS

Now that your recipe is almost complete, let's figure out how to apply this final ingredient to it before you put the cake in the oven. We are going to figure it out by first testing your existing knowledge of what makes a good guy a good guy. Are you already able to point them out? We'll see, yes? Just like before, answer all the questions honestly. If you don't, you won't make the necessary progress required for cooking up that perfect relationship. In addition, I'll highlight my personal answers from high school at the end to clue you in to what I thought made a good guy back then.

1. You get into a fight with your best friend, Molly. You've been really busy lately and haven't been putting a lot of effort into your friendship. She calls you out on it and you aren't very nice to her. You talk about the fight with your boyfriend, giving him both sides of the story. He says:

    a.   You shouldn't worry too much about it. Sometimes people get busy, and if she can't handle it, then that's her problem.

b. Molly is totally right. He has noticed the same thing, and you owe her an apology and a little more effort.

c. You should let the situation cool down for a few days. Then talk to her about it.

2. You and Scott have only been dating for a month when he learns that his parents are coming into town for a visit. You're pretty sure that he has told them about you, and you'd secretly love to meet them. You don't want to pressure him, though, so you don't say anything. He:

a. Makes sure he doesn't mention the exact dates they're coming. He isn't ready to take the next step, even though you are.

b. Conveniently schedules dinner with them when he knows you have class.

c. Tells you that he would feel more comfortable if you met them next time. He really likes you but doesn't want to add the "meeting the parents" pressure quite yet.

3. You've been dating Jeff for about three months, and you notice that when something goes wrong, he gets really angry. Even the smallest things tend to set him

off. He winds up in a sour mood for the rest of the day every single time. You're beginning to become frustrated by his reactions, and you decide to talk to him about it. When you do, he:

   a. Sits quietly for a few moments. He is a little shocked that you said something to him. He tells you that he'd rather not talk about it.

   b. His ears turn red and he sneers that he doesn't know what you're talking about. After a few minutes of silence, he brings it up to you and tells you that he doesn't really know why he angers so easily but that he has always been this way.

   c. Freaks out. He says that you are overly sensitive and that no one has ever said anything like this to him before.

4. You haven't been getting along very well with your mom lately. You keep fighting over little things that didn't used to matter. You don't understand why she has suddenly become so sensitive. You ask your boyfriend what he thinks you should do. He tells you:

   a. That she loves you no matter what. He is sure that it'll pass.

   b. That you are definitely right. Your mom is acting pretty crazy for no reason.

c. That there must be a reason she keeps getting upset with you. He advises you to talk to her about it and listen. What she says may surprise you.

5. You know that the guy you are dating has traditionally gone for girls with long dark brown hair. Yours is blond and shoulder length. To surprise him, you decide to dye it darker and put in some long extensions. When he sees you for the first time, this is his reaction:

   a. *Sexy!*

   b. *Sexy!* But he liked your blond hair, too.

   c. Why did you do that?

6. Sam has been flirting with you at school for ages. He teases you in homeroom almost every morning, and he finds little reasons to come up to you at lunch. It's clear that he is into you, and you like him back. He's never asked for your number, but when he finally does you are ecstatic. When you give it to him, you're so excited that you blurt out, "So, are we going on a date or what?" He laughs it off and gives you a quick hug good-bye. You sit by the phone, waiting for him to call, text, e-mail, anything! Any form of contact is desired. He does text, and it says:

   a. "Miss me already?"

b. "Have plans this weekend? You should get a
    group of your girls together for Friday night."

c. "So . . . what about that date?"

7. Your birthday is coming up in a few days. You haven't
    really made any plans but you're sure a dinner or some-
    thing small can be thrown together at the last minute.
    When you get home from class that evening, you walk
    into your apartment and . . . *surprise!* Your birthday
    party is rocking and rolling, waiting for you to show up
    and celebrate! How did it go down?

    a. Your best girlfriends tell you they planned it
        and that your boyfriend agreed to get in on
        the fun. His job was to pick you up from class
        and take you immediately home. No detours
        for dinner allowed.

    b. You walk in and see all your friends smiling
        at you. Your boyfriend is there too, having a
        drink with his buddies in the kitchen.

    c. Turns out your friends asked your boyfriend
        to help them plan it. He was happy to help,
        and made sure to order your favorite kind of
        cake and flowers for the party.

8. You've always been the kind of girl who makes fun of
    people who do the whole PDA thing. You think it's a

little over the top, but then again, a little hand holding and some sporadic kisses may not be so bad. You tell your boyfriend, who hasn't gone so far as to touch you in public, how you feel about being a little more affectionate.

    a.   He tells you he's never really tried because you never seemed interested. He'd be happy to hold your hand now that he knows that's how you feel.

    b.   He says he has never been comfortable with PDA. You'll just have to suck it up and wait for those treasured kisses to be delivered in private.

    c.   He says he isn't totally comfortable with PDA. A week later, though, he makes that first attempt at hand holding.

9. You're writing a paper for biology. Bio just happens to be the major of the guy you've been dating for a few weeks. You aren't totally secure with what you've written so far, and you ask if he'd mind proofreading it. He says no problem and tells you to e-mail it over. He:

    a.   Sends it back to you the next day. It has some positive notes on the side and some critical edits as well. He asks you to further explain a cell mutation process but adds that your idea gives strength to the paper.

b. He doesn't mention it to you for a few days. When you ask him about it, he scrambles. He sends it back to you with grammar edits and nothing else.

c. He discusses your idea with you. He suggests that you write about cell therapy instead of cell mutation.

10. You and Charlie are still getting to know each other, but you have a dating schedule locked down. For the past three weeks, you've spent every Friday night together at exotic restaurants a town over from campus. Like clockwork, Friday night rolls around and he picks you up at seven o'clock. You:

a. Go to dinner again, just the two of you. He again takes you far from campus to a random restaurant. He says that he wants to explore the city with you, but you aren't so sure anymore.

b. Have a quick bite, then go to his apartment just like last week. He wants to watch a movie and you notice that his roommates aren't there again.

c. Have a quick bite, then go back to his

apartment. His roommates are having a party, and he hopes you don't mind meeting them for the first time under not-normal circumstances.

THE RESULTS

1. a-1, b-3, **c-2**
2. a-2, **b-1**, c-3
3. a-2, b-3, **c-1**
4. **a-2**, b-1, c-3
5. a-2, **b-3**, c-1
6. **a-1**, b-2, c-3
7. **a-2**, b-1, c-3
8. a-3, b-1, **c-2**
9. a-3, **b-1**, c-2
10. a-1, b-2, **c-3**

*The high school version of me scored 18 points, and I would have fallen into the first category below.

WHAT YOUR SCORE MEANS
10–18 POINTS: UM, YOU'RE PICKING LOSERS

I'm sorry, sweetie, but WTF? You're picking complete suckers. These guys are treating you like dog poo, and you either (a) do nothing about it or (b) don't realize that they're treating you like dog poo. Both cases are very depressing. First and foremost, I think that girls should be confident enough to stick up for themselves if they sense something is up. If you know that someone is treating you badly and you don't do anything about it, there is a bigger issue we need to discuss. No one, and I mean no one, is allowed to treat you badly. You do not have to put up with it. If you're scared to make a change, talk to a responsible adult who can help you.

The high school version of me would fall into this group because I was so carefree about guys that if a guy was a jerk to me, I'd simply dump him. I was sometimes a jerk back, and it all boils down to me being an insecure sixteen-year-old. Just because I was "cool" didn't mean I had to say no to real relationships with real emotions. Feeling emotions doesn't make you less of a person. In fact, it makes you a better one.

19–25: Hmm . . .

You have a sense of right and wrong, but sometimes it's the wrong guys who pull you in anyway. You like a little bit of a chase, which is fun and fine, but it's likely that you're chasing guys who don't really care. It's just as easy to pick a nice guy as it is to pick a lame one, and then fill the nice one in on your desire to play hard to get. Simply saying "Babe, you don't always have to be so available to me" with a sly wink will do the trick.

If this isn't the case, you're still figuring out what people are all about. You're discovering that not everyone deserves your trust. But a lot of people do. It just requires you to pick wisely based on what you already know. Utilize the big, beautiful brain that I know you have.

26–30: Yay! You Dig the Good Guys

Woohoo, woohoo, woohoo. Just like you understand what makes a good friend, you understand what makes a good boyfriend. The qualities are essentially the same; it's just the relationship that's different. You're picking guys that you know to be kind, thoughtful, compassionate and trustworthy. In addition, these guys look for the same qualities in you, and because you possess them they love you for who you are. Both sides understand that it's quality over quantity. All I can say is, keep it up!

TYPES OF GUYS: THE GOOD ONES

You know where this is heading. As promised, here is my list of the Good Guys. Each type of Good Guy gives off clear signals that he is the sort of person you should give your time to. Chances are, if you treat him nicely he will respond in kind. In order for a good guy to give you his heart, he needs to know that you rock too.

A side note about good guys: Sometimes the good guys don't fit into that "cool guy" image. Sometimes they're the guys you don't give a chance or a second thought to. Maybe they're a little dorky or a little funny looking—like he's still growing into his ears. Just for now, ladies, just for now. Remember that looks always fade and the dorks go on to start companies like Microsoft.

Part of being a good guy (and you being a good person, too) is looking beyond what others judge to be cool. This is an important lesson to learn now. If you don't, you'll miss out on a lot of the most excellent people you'll ever have the chance to know. Trust me, at twenty it doesn't matter who was "cool" in high school. It just doesn't carry the weight that it once did, before you realized it doesn't really matter. Being "cool" won't get you a job, or a boyfriend or guarantee a nice life.

At twenty it's hard work and love that turn a relationship into a special one. It's likely that these qualities will materialize more easily from a good guy than from one whose only redeeming quality is his muscle tone.

If it turns out that your good guy is superhot, popular, and exceedingly kind, rejoice. You've landed yourself an Adonis. If the good guy who likes you doesn't fit into the perfectly chiseled mold of the man you envision for yourself, give him a chance. Hopefully you'll realize sooner rather than later that it's the stuff inside that really counts.

CONSIDERATE CLAY

Considerate Clay is a breath of fresh air. He is confident in himself, his abilities, and his interest in you. Clay is the kind of guy who wins the "Best Friend" category in your yearbook, and for good reason. He has proven himself to his friends, his teachers, the old lady on the bus—and very soon, to you!

Considerate Clay sees the good in people and also recognizes that flaws make a person unique. He was taught at a young age to use his manners and what using your manners actually does for a person. He has experienced both sides of consideration from people, and that's why he will treat you nicely as well.

Considerate Clay doesn't have to go over the top to show his affection for you. He will do simple things, like bring you flowers out of the blue and ask you how your family is doing. He understands that small gestures count, and he does them with sincerity.

Considerate Clay does like to take care of people, and if there is a situation that you don't need help with, talk to him about it sensitively. He just wants to be there for you, but make sure he understands that you are capable of getting out there on your own, too. If you approach him in the right way, he will respect your independence and be thankful he doesn't have to carry you along.

LIFELONG LIAM

Liam is your lifelong guy friend. You know, the guy you played with while you were both still in diapers. You've grown up together and your families are close too. He knows all your secrets and you know his.

Despite his experience with other girls, you represent something different to him. Because you have such a deep history with Liam, he respects you in a different way from other women. This is not to say that Liam considers you to be one of the family or like a sister. He simply has loved you long enough as a friend that if he became interested in you romantically (and why wouldn't he?), he would be much more inclined to continue treating you like the princess you are.

Liam has been your lifelong friend for good reason. He is dependable. He has been there for you when you've been down. He gives you a guy's point of view whenever you bug him to do so. You understand who the other person is without judgment. Why? Because it's always been that way between the two of you.

Liam has never seen you as anyone other than who you are, and he would never want you to change. All you have to work on now is taking your friendship to a different level.

OLDER OSCAR

When I talk about all the fabulousness that comes along with dating Older Oscar, please make note that I am not talking about really old dudes. That's gross. Older Oscar is a few years older than you are, not twenty-five-plus. I have a truly hard time believing that all those playmates dig Hugh Hefner for his smooth skin and chiseled abs. Likewise, I have a hard time believing that Old Hef dates nineteen-year-olds for their wisdom and breadth of knowledge.

Rather than finding yourself in a pervy situation like the aforementioned, Older Oscar provides the kind of relationship you are ready for. You may be young, but you have a more mature outlook on relationships than, say, most of the guys your age. It's just how Mother Nature decided it would be. Oscar has already made it through his party-guy years and is more inclined to settle down now with the right girl. It's essentially a perfect match between you two: Despite the slight difference in age, you're in the same relationship space. You desire a more mature relationship, and he has the experience and willingness to provide it.

However, if you find yourself dating Older Oscar, be careful to stick to what you know is right. His expectations may be different from yours (especially physically) so it's important to discuss "where this is going" with him. It would be foolish to jump into a serious relationship with Oscar simply because you're both ready. He has to be the right guy for you. If he isn't, the relationship you're both ready for will never last.

WORKIN' WILL

We all know Workin' Will. He is not only quarterback of the football team and student body president, he also has a 4.0 GPA and aspires to finish Yale Law by the time he is twenty-five. Some girls may worry that Will won't ever have time for them in his busy schedule, but it's just a matter of winning his heart.

Clearly, Will is driven. He loves to feel accomplished, and he is proud of everything that he works so hard to do. What drives this passion in Will? Whether he recognizes this animalistic instinct in himself or not, he is passionate because he wants to be a great provider for his family. This is the reason that Will can make room in his busy schedule for an equally competent female: you. He needs the girl to complete his life puzzle.

In a girl, Will is essentially looking for his diligent counterpart. Not to say that you have to like the same things he does and follow the same career path. No way! But Will does want a girl who is just as motivated and driven as he is. Lying around all day while Will brings home the bacon will not fly. He wants his lady to admire and appreciate his zeal so that he can appreciate hers in return.

GLEEFUL GREG

Gleeful Greg probably isn't your next boyfriend, but he is a great guy to have a lot of fun with. Why isn't he your next boyfriend? He just isn't ready yet. In this case, though, it doesn't mean that Greg is one of the Baddies. Just like it's taken you time to develop, Greg deserves that chance too without automatically being labeled a jerk.

Gleeful Greg is so enjoyable to be around because he is truly happy. He sees the positive in everything rather than the negative. He turns a regular day at the mall into an exuberant afternoon of rifling through the masks at your little brother's favorite toy store. He livens up a low-energy get-together in an instant. He turns your frown upside down with a quick joke and a squeeze of the arm.

Greg has these qualities because, at the end of the day, he is a nice guy. Only nice people are able to see the good in almost every situation. This means that for now, let Greg have his fun and don't hesitate to take part in it yourself. The day he is ready for a relationship, expect it to be one full of fun, love, and laughter.

MONOGAMOUS MIKE

Monogamy isn't optional for Mike, it's a way of life. He understands on a very basic level why it's important to remain faithful to the person you love. The reasons? First, because you do love them, and you should never intentionally hurt the people you care for. Second, because cheating breaks the trust between a guy and a girl. Trust is the foundation of all successful relationships. Without it, what else do you have?

Most likely, Monogamous Mike has learned this lesson from a firsthand experience. Maybe Mike has been cheated on, so he knows the pain of being on the receiving end. Or maybe Mike has been the cheater. In his case, though, just like kids learn important lessons at a young age, Mike learned his lesson and isn't making that mistake again. There's also the possibility that Mike's parents went through a divorce as a result of infidelity. Children learn quickly from this that cheating is never the right answer. They see how it tears families apart, and they frequently vow to never cheat.

Whatever the case, Mike is looking forward to being faithful to you. He knows that the bond faithfulness will create between you is better than the feelings you get from cheating. And more often than not, most guys are the Monogamous Mike type. It's unfortunate that a lot of guys have to prove themselves to be good, just because other idiots out there are messing it up.

If you're dating a new guy, talk to him about monogamy early on. If you make your feelings known right away, the chances that your guy won't find himself being led astray are much higher. And Monogamous Mike is sincere when he tells you he'll never cheat. You can hear it in his voice, see it in his face, and understand that it's an issue you'll never have to worry about.

CHARITABLE CASEY

Charitable Casey is someone you will always be able to rely on. Why? He is happy enough with himself that it leads him to help other people in return. He is the guy who commandeers a food drive at your school every single Thanksgiving without fail. When the holidays roll around, he'll get a group of friends together to gather up toys in his neighborhood for families in need. He walks dogs every Sunday at the local shelter. He coaches a youth soccer team. He helps his mom with the dishes every night. He drives his sister to piano lessons.

Big or small, the contributions that Casey makes to the lives of the people he loves have a lasting effect on his family and his community. What makes Casey the kind of guy that he is? Compassion. It's a character trait that is hard to come by but extremely valuable. Whenever everyone else loses interest, he continues on with his endeavor.

In a relationship, compassion is an element that turns a partnership into a loving one. Charitable Casey will always be there for you, because he is content with himself. How can you give back to Charitable Casey? Always believe in him. It's his sense of self that allows him to go so far for others, and when you reinforce who he is, he'll care for you that much more.

ADVISABLE AARON

Advisable Aaron is a guy who's comfortable enough in his own skin that he is able to take advice rather than respond to it with anger. You know the angry types, too, right? Kindly mention something you notice and they respond like they've already handled what you're talking about, or else they'll get confrontational and dismissive. Don't these guys get that you're not trying to be a bother, you're simply trying to help?

Aaron gets it. The reason he gets it, though, is that he knows you are smart enough to warrant him taking some tips from you here and there. He really trusts and values your opinion because you have been there for him over and over again. Advisable Aaron takes what you think into account so seriously that sometimes what you think is the deciding factor for him.

He appreciates what you have to say because you have proven yourself to him. He likes that you have a strong opinion and know yourself well enough to know what that opinion is. He also values the fact that you are willing to take advice from him sometimes too. It's just the kind of girl you are.

FIRST-BOYFRIEND BEN

Aww, the sweet bliss of First-Boyfriend Ben. You're Ben's first girlfriend, and that makes you very special indeed. He has been feeling like he's ready, and he has finally found the right girl to take that first leap of faith with.

Don't worry if Ben seems a little shy about some things and dives headfirst into others. Just like you, he has a fantasy of what his first romantic relationship should be, and if he buys you flowers out of the blue, you've found yourself one delightful first love. You're paired up with a guy who is figuring it out but wants to test out all the sweet things he has conjured up for you.

Make sure to surprise Ben back when he does something sweet for you. This will make Ben feel like you value him and your relationship just as much as he does. It's bound to keep your first love fresh and lighthearted, just like it's meant to be.

TYPES OF RELATIONSHIPS:
THE GOOD ONES

Speaking of first boyfriends, the first relationship story I'm going to tell is about just that. And it's a good one! Finally, just as we moved from describing the Baddies to the Goodies, we get to progress from tales of bad relationships into good ones. Romantic relationships should do nothing but make you feel good—about yourself, your partner, and the life you share together.

If you've never had a boyfriend, these stories will demonstrate to you what a good relationship looks like. It will teach you how good boyfriends and girlfriends treat each other. If you've had sucky relationships, you'll see why these are different and how you can apply what's being described here to your own life. If you already have an exceptional connection to a boy, it's just fun to read other people's stories. Chances are, they'll reinforce what you already know to be true.

I don't think this section needs any more of an introduction, so let's get right to it. The stories you'll read are about three harmonious partnerships. Two of the stories belong to dear friends of mine, Penny and Liz, and the third story is my own. Enjoy!

PENNY AND BEAU

Penny and Beau met on the job, a true office romance. The location? A well-known production studio in the Valley. Penny had her dream job, working in TV development, and Beau was an up-and-comer in the marketing department. Beau was a few years older than Penny and a few positions above her, and their relationship started out as a professional one. But one thing led to another, then professional turned friendly and friendly turned flirtatious.

Penny is my age, and she has long blond hair and great taste. She's always wearing something unique, an outfit you could pull from the pages of *W* or *Vanity Fair*. If I were to describe Penny in one word, I would choose "chic." It took her a while to come into this identity, though. Not that she hasn't always been chic (chic girls are born that way), she just tried a little bit of everything before deciding on this identity over all the others. Some days she was a hipster, other days she was grunge. The following Saturday she was the preppy girl from high school, and the next day it was back to high fashion. With each look came a different passion: Dreams of producing records to planning weddings rotated around in her fantasy life.

This unfettered self-discovery defined Penny in recent years. She was constantly moving between one thing or another, figuring out what she liked best and what drove her. Despite her many passions, there's always been a constant in Penny's life: Land the dream job and the dream guy.

Constantly inspired and changing her mind, it took Penny a while to accomplish her two consistent goals. When she finally picked television over all the other fields she had an interest in, it was a scary decision for her. TV is hard, no matter if you're in front of the camera or behind it. She took the leap, though, and found herself extremely happy with her decision. She finally felt comfortable in one aspect of her life. She was good at her job, and it fulfilled her creative needs every single day.

Next came the dream guy. Of course the dream job and amazing guy would go hand in hand for a girl like Penny. She always wanted both, and it was just her luck that they would come in a pair. Beau noticed Penny before she noticed him. Every day at one o'clock, she would walk by his office on her way to lunch. Once Beau realized who she was, he made sure not to leave until Penny had just walked past his door. This gave him the opportunity to catch up to her and ask her out to lunch. At first she was hesitant. Being more than "just friends" with a coworker was not exactly in her grand plan. She figured she would be friendly, though, and take him up on his offer.

They ended up hitting it off instantly. Right away, Penny knew she had never connected with a guy like she was connecting with Beau. He was cool, he loved TV, and he loved that she loved it too. He was just as passionate as she was about it, which only reinforced her decision to work there in the first place. Other guys she had known weren't always as supportive. They thought she would be better suited to being a party planner. Something girlier, she always guessed.

The fact that Penny actually liked Beau made her nervous. Despite her bright personality, she had never had a real boyfriend before. It's not like boys weren't into Penny, because she had certainly experienced a few here and there. It's just that she wasn't into the guys who paid attention to her. There was always something a little off about them to her.

Truth be told, all the guys who had ever liked Penny enjoyed spending time with her because she was spontaneous and different. Penny didn't love her spontaneity, though; she was much more comfortable when she'd pinned down who she was. The quality that guys loved about her but made Penny feel queasy always ruined whatever shot they had together. She just wasn't sure who she was yet, so she didn't want to get into a relationship she wasn't into on top of it.

By the time she met Beau, though, she had figured it out. She was a chic, smart, junior development exec! And she was ready for that first boyfriend. For years she had seen her friends have success with guys, and she knew it was her turn to experience that as well.

They transitioned easily from coworkers into more than that. Because Beau was older, he was ready for a relationship just as much as Penny was. They jumped right in, and the day Beau asked Penny to be his girlfriend, she said yes.

Like any couple, after their first month or two, they had their first fight. Because they worked together, they frequently attended the same social events thrown by their office at night. Sometimes Beau was obligated to go to a work event and would invite Penny because he desperately wanted to see her. In return, she felt like he wasn't making enough of an effort to spend time with her apart from work. It angered Penny, and Beau sensed it.

What secured their relationship is how they handled the dispute. Rather than letting it boil, Beau brought it up with Penny the next day at work. He asked her how she felt about hanging out at work events, giving her the opportunity to speak her mind. She took it, and instead of getting angry or hurting each other's feelings over a measly party, they figured out a schedule that would work for both of them.

Because they approached their first squabble in a mature way, it laid the foundation for the rest of their relationship. Whenever something was brewing between them, it only took one person to acknowledge what was going on for the other to openly talk about it. They just clicked in this way, and their ability to handle disputes kept their relationship strong despite that, as with any relationship, they are two different, independently thinking people.

In the spring, Beau asked Penny to go on a camping trip with him. He wasn't sure how Penny would respond. She definitely is a girl who prefers to sleep indoors, away from the bugs and the dirt. But Penny was up for the challenge, mostly because she was excited to do something that Beau wanted to do. As insignificant as it might seem to others, taking a trip that Beau was wild about further solidified their relationship. Beau knew this, and it confirmed for him what he already knew he felt. The first night together, safe from the bugs in their tent, Beau told Penny that he loved her. First boyfriend, first camping trip, first love.

LIZ AND BRETT

Here is the lo-down (ha!) on Liz and Brett. Their history is important, of course, but the focus in this story is how their relationship went from being an average one to being a special one.

Liz and Brett met at a Fourth of July party two years ago. She had seen him around town a little bit, and Brett had definitely noticed Liz. She's the kind of girl you simply can't ignore. Hot body, hot face, hot brain. The total package. What more could you ask for?

They hit it off right away. They had similar personalities and were drawn to each other through their desires to never let a moment pass them by. They loved to surprise each other with adventures: skydiving one day, a night at the ballet the next, followed by fishing in Cabo. The world was their oyster and they took every opportunity to live it up together.

All these experiences taught Liz and Brett a lot about each other. Liz, despite sometimes coming off as girly girl, was truly adventurous at heart. Brett, though he put forward a huge personality, was more sensitive and kind than Liz initially realized. They enjoyed both the time spent they together and the people they were with each other. They were a good match.

Liz had always judged her relationships based on a few things: how well they got along, if they both preferred spicy tuna rolls over salmon, and how soon her boyfriend met her family and vice versa. Being the decisive girl she was, she soon invited Brett to meet her family. Brett happily agreed, secretly thrilled that Liz liked him enough to take this step, and the entire family went out to dinner a week later.

Of course, Brett and her family got along fabulously. As always, Liz felt even more confident in her relationship once her boyfriend had met her parents. She had yet to meet Brett's family, though, and they only lived fifteen minutes away.

And Brett went home a lot. Sometimes once a week, or every other week, just to catch up with his family and say hi. Liz noticed how frequently he did this and waited patiently for her invitation to meet his family. It didn't come, though, and it started to bother her. Whenever he went home, Liz was immediately thrown into a sour mood. She interpreted the nonexistent invitation as a clear indicator that he was not into her as much as she liked him.

But despite what Liz thought, Brett absolutely adored her. She was the first girl he saw having a real future with. He loved her, and he knew that one day Liz would meet his family. Before this happened, though, he wanted enough time to tell his parents all about her: her accomplishments, what they had done that day, the sweet thing she had done for him last week. Why? Because the first and only time he had brought a girl home, his mother informed him later that she wasn't a huge fan. This tore Brett apart, and it eventually led to the destruction of that relationship.

He didn't want this to be the case with Liz, even though he knew that Liz was completely different from the other girl. Liz had character, a personality, strong convictions: all the things his mother wanted for him in a girl. He was simply afraid, and he thought that by not taking her home, he was protecting her.

This continued for a while until Liz reached her breaking point. They got into a fight over it, and Brett realized how much he had been hurting her. He didn't know meeting the family was such a big deal for Liz. She had never said anything about it apart from when he met hers, so he assumed it wasn't an issue. Even more, he thought it was a bigger issue for him than for her. Embarrassed, he explained the issue to Liz and she forgave him once she realized how he felt about it too.

The next week, Liz met Brett's parents. She did her nails, curled her hair, and picked out the appropriate casual-but-not-too-casual outfit. She was nervous. This was a big deal to her! Meeting the parents took a relationship to a totally new, higher, more amazing level. And despite Brett's first, bad experience bringing a girl home, his parents absolutely loved Liz, for all the same reasons that Brett adored her too.

After the meeting, Liz and Brett talked again about what had happened. They realized that they didn't discuss it between them before out of embarrassment and worry created from a past experience. They made a commitment to be open and honest with each other from that day forward regardless of the issues that happened to come up. In turn, their relationship rose to an entirely new level of commitment. Meeting each other's parents had been a success, just as they had both envisioned.

SCOTT AND ME

Scott and I first met at a taping of *American Idol*, the season that brought us the singing sensation Adam GLAMbert. Well, we didn't exactly meet at *American Idol*, but we definitely crossed paths there for the first time. He was seated in front of my girlfriends and me. He had a date with him: his mom.

Pretty cute. I noticed him, and he noticed me. To this day, he tells me he felt an energy between us. I always laugh when he reminds me of this "energy."

The next time we ran into each other was at a small bar in Manhattan Beach. Very limited seating in this place, and the only open spot was next to me. Shamefully enough, I was there with my ex-boyfriend (ha!), and Scott showed up with a girl. Another random encounter, but this time we managed to stop staring at each other and actually say hello. I didn't immediately remember that this was the cute guy whose head had blocked my view of the stage at *Idol*, but he certainly did. We had a brief exchange of words, but enough to learn that it turned out we had had mutual friends for years and years. It just so happened that we had never been in the same place at the same time . . . until now.

By the next time I saw Scott, my previous boyfriend and I had broken up. Our relationship had ended emotionally a while before we actually called it quits, so when Scott and I ran into each other again, I felt fully single and ready to mingle. It happened at my friend Frankie's birthday party. I had sworn to Frankie that I would go to his party, and when none of my girlfriends were able to tag along, I dutifully went alone. And out of the blue, Scott showed up in my path once again.

I felt by now that something weird was going on: The planets had aligned, or some bizarre magnetic force kept bringing us together. Or maybe it was fate. That's what I like to say back to Scott when he talks about our chance *American Idol* encounter. Whatever the case, the third time was the charm.

As it turns out, it was a good thing I went to the party alone that night. I'm absolutely terrified of riding in taxis by myself (unless I'm in New York City—that's a different story), and I thought that my way in with Scott would be to politely ask for a ride home. We had hit it off at the start of the night, so I figured he would say yes. Turns out, he shattered my dreams of the perfect ride home together and said no. *Just kidding*, friends. Of course he said yes. Sometimes you girls are too gullible for your own good.

He gave me a ride home, and that was that. We set sail off into the sunset together forever. Sort of. Scott and I are very comfortable together now, and lucky to have each other. Like any relationship, though, getting to that point took some time.

We got to know each other very quickly because of the quality of conversations we had. I consider myself to be an oldie at heart, a girl who focuses more on the serious side of life than the fleeting aspects of it. Scott is older than I am by a few years, but emotionally at the same place as me. Both of us were ready for a serious relationship but had not quite found the right person to move forward with.

What initially amazed me was that we actually discussed this about ourselves. Here, for the first time in my life, was a guy openly talking to me about the kind of relationships he had before, the kinds of things he learned from them, and the sort of relationship he was looking forward to having with a girl. I responded similarly, comfortable telling him I was ready for the real thing because he was so honest with me about his desires as well.

It's this honesty between us, this ability to talk about anything and everything, that became the foundation for our relationship. I learned from Scott that having an open dialogue with your partner from the get-go is the only way to turn a relationship into a lasting one. It's a good thing we started out this way too, because Scott and I have had our fair share of disagreements.

Our disagreements always start because one of us isn't fully clear on what the other person is saying or doing. I don't mean that we are dishonest about what's going on—this is never the case. Sometimes we simply have a hard time understanding the other's train of thought. We've chalked it up to our brains working in completely contrasting ways. I like to give the example of working out a math problem when I explain this: Different people find the answer through different processes based on the direction their brain sends them in. This is how Scott and I approach everything—by taking different routes to find the answer.

Thankfully, more times than not, we come to the same answer, despite however we got there. It's a blessing to get along with your partner in this way: you feel the same way about most things, even if your way of expressing it is different. And that's where the honesty between us consistently comes into play. I'm comfortable asking him an honest question to figure out what's going on in his head, and he does the same with me. It takes a little work on both our ends to explain the way we are feeling, but once we're clued in to each other, we're on the same page from there on out.

Scott and I also have a deep trust in each other. For a lot of people, trust develops over time. This is partly the case with him and me, but the initial trust between us grew out of types of conversations we had when we began dating. We talked about a lot of the stuff that is sometimes embarrassing to talk about: a fear of being cheated on, what it's like to feel hurt, where we wanted our relationship to go. Instead of regressing because of the things that bothered us, we were honest about them. Scott and I both felt the same way about remaining faithful to each other, and this is something I will never worry about. We had both been hurt by someone we wanted to believe in, and we vowed not to hurt each other in the same ways. We agreed to treat each other with love and respect from the get-go, and it's the most mature relationship decision I have ever made.

The best part about our relationship is that we have the most fun when we are just goofing around together. Serious goofing around—really letting loose, letting your freak flag fly and feeling comfortable in your own weirdness—takes self-confidence. I don't feel like I have to put on the facade of the hot, fashionable girl around Scott. I reserve that girl for the red carpet. Around the house, I prefer to dance in sweatpants to no music with my boyfriend.

I'm comfortable being myself around Scott, and it is something I am thankful for every day. He never makes me feel like I have to compromise the girl I am for him. He loves me for me, and that's more than enough.

When we first started dating, we liked to say to each other, "You are lucky to have me." Now we say to each other, "I'm lucky to have you." I love you.

WHAT IF YOUR FRIENDS
DON'T LIKE HIM?

He has taken you out on a few amazing dates, and it seems like you've met *the* guy so, you think it's about time he came over to your apartment to meet your girlfriends. He obliges, of course (why wouldn't he? You are one hot piece!) and agrees on a night of dinner and TV at home.

He gets there, and the standard introductions are made. You can tell that he is a little nervous because your friends are all so amazing that they blow him away, but he is hanging in there just fine. You show him your bedroom, the one you share with your roommate, and he makes a joke, poking fun at the pile of clothes (hello, standard) in the corner of the room. You and your roommate look at each other, and while you laugh, she flatly says, "They're mine." She leaves the room, and you know that you're in trouble.

The rest of the night goes off without a hitch, minus your grumpy best friend, who retreats to the far corner of the couch for the rest of the night, engrossed in the newest episode of *Grey's Anatomy*. When your Prince Charming hits the road, your best friend turns to you and comments that he is the rudest guy you've ever brought home, and that she really doesn't like him.

Uh-oh. You know he was just making a joke about your bedroom and that his comment shouldn't be taken seriously. Your bestie, on the other hand, thinks he should have kept his mouth shut the first time he came over. She has made up her mind about your new guy, and it's not the reaction you were hoping for.

Does this story sound familiar? It should. Every one of us has brought home a guy who, for some reason or another, is disliked by one of our girlfriends. Some reasons are silly and should be overlooked. I mean, you gave *her* boyfriend a fair shot, right? Right! She should do the same for you.

It doesn't always happen this way, but for the most part, a bad first impression tends to melt away after a group of you spend more time together. Whoever was turned off realizes that the first-encounter snafu was really just a first-encounter snafu, nothing more. It takes a little while to understand a new friend's sense of humor, and misunderstandings are common. If you find yourself in a situation like this, ask your bestie to give him another shot. She should—she is your best friend. And most likely she will, and the group of you will ride off into the sunset together as great friends.

On the other hand, if a friend comes to you with a serious reason why she doesn't approve of your new guy, it's worth considering, but from more points of view than one. First and foremost, consider who this worried friend is. Is she really a good friend of yours, or merely an acquaintance? The level of your friendship should be the first indicator of whether to take what she is saying seriously or not. Sometimes freak girls have a crush on your new boyfriend and try to sabotage your relationship for selfish reasons. I know. Crazy. Gross. You're not that girl.

Sometimes acquaintances happen to know this new guy better than you do. When I dated John, his lifelong friends warned me about him. I figured they were weirdos, so I ignored them. I shouldn't have. Whatever the case may be, do a little research if your informant is not in your inner circle of best girlfriends.

Next, after you've considered the source and deem her sane enough to be taken seriously, consider what she is saying to you. Is her story about her friend who happens to be the ex-girlfriend who cheated on him? Does she tell you he's the most horrible guy ever because he didn't call her friend back for a week after he found out? Or has something completely removed occurred that is more serious than just an ex-girlfriend's leftover jealousy? I'm talking serious in a creepy, really should be talked about kind of way.

If someone you trust ever—and I mean ever—talks to you about any sort of abuse, listen up. Stories about hitting a girl, getting in a fight with someone's brother, getting arrested for selling drugs, and so forth are all types of things that are not simply made up out of thin air. Even if what you're being told is not 100 percent factual, there is something fishy going on. People don't just make up crazy stories about other people. Every story, even ones that are totally out there, start as true in some way. There is a reason that you're being told what you are. And if you find yourself in this situation, run. It's far better to leave a jerk early and easily than to leave him later on, after you find out that what you've been told is true, true, true. When you leave him, don't bother to bring up whatever scary thing he's done. Just say you'd be better off as friends and move on amicably.

If, on the other hand, you hear a story from a trusted friend that isn't frightening but still bothers you in some way, pay attention. All stories come from a place of truth, so they're worth discussing with your new guy.

All in all, it's important to pay attention to what your friends are saying to you about a new relationship. It's equally important to give a fair shot to your new guy. Figure out what is really going on and then side with the person who is being honest with you. But remember, the relationship is yours and yours alone. If a friend simply doesn't get along with him, that's not a good enough reason to call it quits. Be strong for yourself, whether that means listening to your friends or listening to your heart.

TEN INITIAL SIGNS THAT HE LIKES YOU

There are some easy clues a guy will give to indicate he likes you. You just have to be cognizant enough to identify them. Just in case you've been living in a hole, here are ten initial signs that he *is into you*. Besides these first ten, anything he does to make you feel warm and tingly inside can essentially be taken as a sign.

1. **He asks you on a date**. Yes, this may seem obvious, but if he isn't asking you out, he still isn't completely sure how he feels about you. A guy who is serious about you will man up and do it.
2. **He texts you . . . a lot.** Your friends and your

mom text you a lot, but when you throw a guy into that cell phone mix, it's a sign that he loooooooves you. If he texts the same night after your first date, you get bonus points.

3. **He asks you out again.** This seems as obvious as number one. If he does not ask you to hang with him again, it probably didn't go as stellar the first time as you thought. If he continues to text you but doesn't make that critical next move, ask him if he wants to meet up at your friend's party this weekend. If he is wishy-washy about it, you have your answer right there. Time to move on.

4. **He tells you something private.** Any guy you're dating who is willing to trust you with something private is into you. No need to worry about what he is feeling. He is showing you through his actions.

5. **He touches you.** Calm down, pervs. Not like that. I mean, he touches you on places like your arm, the small of your back, your hand. Any guy who is into you can't help himself. He is magnetically drawn to you, and the slightest brush of skin is mind blowing.

6. **He does something silly**. If he does something silly but cute, *he is into you*. Frequently these

"silly" things resemble small gifts of some kind, from a text message pic of a cute stuffed animal (digital gift, ha) to the real thing. Whatever it is will most likely have a small amount of meaning, probably from an inside joke or something along those lines.

7. **He introduces you to his friends.** Yes, the male friend introduction is very important and one of the clearest signs he will give off. If he likes you a lot, he will introduce you to his friends. Guys tend to joke around with one another, especially about girls, so if he is willing to take the jovial heat from them for you, you're golden.

8. **He gives you a nickname.** If he gives you a pet name, he likes you. My boyfriend started to call me LoLo (not too original, but cute nonetheless) after knowing me a few days. Babe, baby, sweetness, sugarlips, superwoman, etcetera all count as well.

9. **He responds if you text.** Like many of the others, this one seems obvious, but it's a true sign. Frequently there is a lot of texting back and forth during the early days of a relationship. Sometimes you make it a point not to text him, just to see if he'll text you! He is

playing the exact same game you are, sweetie. Let him win every once in a while, though, and just send him the first text. If he responds all over the place, that's a sign!

10. **He lets you into his social space.** By social space, I mean his online social network, such as Facebook, Twitter, or MySpace. If he asks for your friendship or follows you—or whatever it is that kids are doing these days—he is sharing his interest in you with the entire world. Take it as a compliment and a sign.

KEEPING YOUR COOL

We all know how easy it is to think OMG, OMG, OMG when a guy first lets you know he likes you. So fun, right? Yes, of course. Realizing that the guy you are crushing on likes you back is absolutely, positively so much fun. It's an amazing feeling and one you should revel in. There is something to be said, however, for keeping your cool.

This is what I mean by keeping your cool: internalizing the OMGs to some degree whenever you interact with your hot, new future husband. Girls always ask me why they should hide their true feelings from the guy they like, and I tell them that keeping your cool is not hiding what you're feeling. Keeping your cool is a way to finesse your excitement into something desirable rather than something a little too crazy for words.

Guys, by nature, are always, without a doubt, a little freaked out if the girl they are digging comes on too strongly. Why? Not because he did a 180 and decides he doesn't like you anymore but because showing too much emotion, interest, whatever, indicates to the guy that you are ready to get serious right away. He wants to get serious too, but he needs to be more sure of it. His reasoning behind this is that if he approaches the situation slowly and rationally, he has taken the steps to protect himself from getting hurt. Yes, guys have feelings too. Bottom line: He is afraid to dive right in.

Girls, on the other hand, are full of emotion and go with their instincts. Keeping your cool creates a balance between being too rational and too emotional. This balance will let your guy know that you are into him but that you're going about it in the same way he is.

Keeping your cool in no way changes how you feel or who you are. You are simply manipulating your behavior to keep *the chase* interesting. The guy took you out on the first date because he already knows that *you* are interesting. No need to worry about that. The chase is a different story.

The chase provides you with the opportunity to show the guy you like how real and levelheaded you really are, rather than blowing it right away and falsely indicating that you are an emotional heavy hitter. Give too much away and watch what you know could be great fizzle out after date number one. Keep your cool and make the leap from first-date girl to second-date girl.

So, how do you keep your cool?

- **Keep quiet.** There is no real need to run your mouth all over town about how much you L-O-V-E your new guy. Chances are, someone you don't want knowing will hear and R-U-I-N it for you.
- **Respond in moderation.** Do not text or call this guy one hundred times a day if he is not doing the same to you. That's creepy. You're blowing it. When he texts or calls you, do a private jump for joy, wait five minutes, and then respond accordingly.
- **Turn him down.** This is one of the most powerful things a girl can do, so don't be afraid to utilize it. Turn him down every once in a while. It's not going to be the end of the world. Turning him down to hang with your girlfriends lets him know that you aren't the kind of girl who will just roll over. Make him work for it.
- **Don't tag.** Absolutely do not tag the guy you are just starting to date in your Facebook pictures. More often than not, he will feel like you are staking a claim to him in a very public

arena. And admit it, that's exactly what you're trying to do. This also applies to wall messages and tweets. A message here or there is not the end of the world, but try to keep your love notes and photos private.

PART 4

BUILDING YOUR RELATIONSHIP

HELLO, HOT STUFF. NOT ONLY DO YOU KNOW THAT YOU'RE AN amazing student, beautiful daughter, party queen, ab flexer, top chef, and friend, you have a foxy boyfriend to match. When people ask you how you got so lucky, you reply, "It's not luck, sweetie. It's just me."

Having it all feels good, right? Right! And now that you have it all, you have to face the reality that you will have to continue to work at it in order to maintain it. No problem, though: You've already put in enough time getting to this wonderful place that keeping it up is a breeze. It just takes a little creativity and a lot of love.

Creativity and love: Both make you feel really nice inside. They are also required for relationships that have life beyond the six-month mark. Why? Because, as anyone who has had a long-term relationship knows, those initial feelings of infatuation tend to fade. What is important to acknowledge, however is that the fading of the initial tingly feelings simply means they are transforming into solid ones for your partner. And which would you prefer? Tinglies that, while fun, represent an uncertain future, or solid feelings that represent a real commitment? The right answer? Solid feelings, duh. The tinglies don't even embody feelings of love, anyway. The tinglies are pure adrenaline. Don't get me wrong, I'm not hating on the tinglies. Everyone enjoys them, including myself. I'm just trying to make sure you understand the difference, so you don't get down on your relationship when the newness of it wears off in exchange for comfort.

Comfort, or being comfortable with your boyfriend, allows for far better experiences together than what you felt getting to know each other initially, because you are secure enough to let loose. Comfort allows you to properly build your relationship into a long-term one. That's where the creativity and love come back into play. There are a lot of tips in the following pages on how to accomplish this powerful combination. Because you know each other well, it takes a creative effort driven by love to keep your relationship feeling brand-spanking-new over time. For example, scheduling a weekly date night is a good way to make sure you are spending time together—that's the love part. The creative part is mixing up what you're doing, to make sure you're really enjoying each other's company. It's easier than you think to get out of the dinner-and-a-movie date rut. Just use your imagination! The payoff is worth it. And once you actually experience this for yourself, you'll see that building your relationship provides the best of both worlds: the merriment of a new relationship combined with the ease of a mature one.

In order to get to the point where your relationship goes from fling to serious, it's important to reflect on why this change is occurring. Think about it: you've proven yourself to your guy and he's proven himself to you. You are comfortable being yourself around him, and he is too. You trust each other. Because you believe in yourself, you allow yourself to believe in him as well.

I've been preaching it for more than 160 pages now, and I'll say it again: The strength of your relationship depends on how much you believe in it and in yourself (remember that Golden Rule, darlings!). It starts with personal belief—knowing that you are deserving of a great relationship. Then it moves into belief in your partner, and finally takes the form of a partner- ship as you come to believe in what you have with that person. Once you reach boyfriend-girlfriend status, you start to build on what you already have confidence in.

Maintaining a long-term relationship may seem daunting at times. It's this fear, though, the fear of potentially losing a relationship, that causes some relationships to go stale. You can't allow yourself to be wrapped up in the what-ifs. Instead, focus on the present and the undeniable fact that you are strong enough to do it right. You love yourself and you love your boyfriend, and when you love someone, you allow them to see you as the person you really are. It's by being your uninhibited self that you will learn how to build upon a relationship that seemingly cannot get any bigger or better. I'll say it again: *You must lose your inhibitions around your partner* to experience long-term relationship success. What better person to do this with, though? You already trust your boyfriend, so why not let him see the *real* real you (I'm thinking sweatpants and zero makeup)?

When you lose your inhibitions, you let down your wall to expose an even more private part of yourself to a guy who desires to know *this* person. Chances are, it will be a little scary at first, but it's through this exploration of the real you that you two will continue to build upon what you already have, and the building process itself can be a really enjoyable experience.

Turn exploring your inhibitions into a creative way to have fun with your boyfriend. If you've secretly always wanted to be a pastry chef, take cooking classes together. Always dreamed of making out in the snow? Do it! Do it with him! It only takes a moment of uncertainty to reveal that thing you've always wanted to do with him, but once you do it, it's out there for good. Chances are, he'd love to explore the Costa

Rican rain forest with you or help you put together a plan for your dream business.

It's experiencing these tender, important moments together that will both make them memorable and commit you to each other even more. You will trust each other on a deeper level, knowing that you've shared something important. Your belief in him will increase because he supported your ideas to stir up a little fun between the two of you.

Support his creativity as well. He is confident enough in you to reveal a part of himself that perhaps no one else will get the pleasure of knowing. So, remember: Creativity + Love = A Relationship Built to Last.

QUIZ: IS IT MUTUAL?

Before we dive headfirst into all the lovey-dovey stuff you and your boyfriend will do together, I want to interject a teeny, tiny reality check. Sometimes when you're so engrossed in each other it's important to take a minor step back and confirm what you know to be true. Are you guys feeling intimacy on the same level? In other words, is it mutual?

There are some ways to determine if you are for real and if he is for real. Hopefully you're *both* for real about each other, so do us all a favor (mostly yourself) and answer a few questions before we proceed. I'll tell you again, and I'll keep on saying it: Be honest with your answers. You'll only learn what's really going on if you tell the truth!

1. You and your new guy have tentative plans to hang out Thursday night. It's his only night off, and he mentioned wanting to hang out with you. Your girlfriends call Thursday morning and invite you to the coolest party ever. You really want to go. How does it play out?

    a. He tells you it's totally fine, as long as you promise to make some time for him this weekend!

    b. Your girlfriends tell you to invite your guy after you reveal you have plans with him. You invite him, and he tells you to have fun with your girls.

    c. You feel so bad that you even considered ditching your boyfriend, you hang with him and make no mention of the party.

2. Your boyfriend has a really great new job, but it means he can't always be by his cell phone. You, on the other hand, cling to your BlackBerry as if it's life or death and send him a few messages every day anyway. After a few days of him being at the new gig, you get into a communication routine. What's it like?

    a. He dutifully calls you at one thirty every day, during his lunch break, to thank you for all the sweet messages.

    b. He responds to all your messages right away,

even if it means slacking off some of the time.

c. He rarely acknowledges all the funny e-mails you send. Sometimes he is so tired after work he doesn't say anything about them for a day or two.

3. Rob, your new stud of a boyfriend, really loves to play basketball. He plays on the team at school, but his favorite game is every Saturday with his friends. You know about it because you've been dating for a while, but you have yet to go watch him. When you ask him if you can, he says:

a. "Baby, just come to my games at school. Those are the important ones."

b. "It would be so sweet if you came. I've been wondering if you wanted to come at all."

c. "Sweetie, it's not a real game, but if you want to come watch, I'd love to have you there."

4. A group of your friends hang out every Saturday night. Your boyfriend has become part of the crew, and it always turns into a long night discussing what's going on with everyone. One of your girlfriends recounts a story about a date she went on recently. The guy was a real jerk and ended up hitting on another girl at the bar they went to after dinner. Everyone has a different opinion

about what happened. You tell her that the guy is a total wase of time. After that, your boyfriend says:

 a. "Yep, what a loser," even though the guy is a lifelong friend of his.

 b. "He's my friend. I don't think he's a waste of time."

 c. "I know him pretty well, and it seems out of character for him. I'm sorry it happened that way."

5. Bobby, the sweet guy you've been seeing for a few weeks, seems sort of down in the dumps. You ask him what's wrong, and he tells you that he's having a hard time getting an internship. Every interview he goes on emphasizes his inexperience in the field rather than all the stuff he is really good at. How do you handle it?

 a. You surprise him the next night with a delicious homemade dinner and a great movie.

 b. You surprise him with dinner, and as a thank-you he takes you to Santa Barbara for the entire day that weekend.

 c. You surprise him with dinner. He says thanks, but he watches TV while he is eating and doesn't help with the dishes.

6. Out of nowhere, you and your guy get into your first fight. It's nothing major, but it's the first time you've been angry with each other. After a fight, it's pretty normal to make up, and part of making up is recommitting to your boyfriend. A lot of couples do this by verbalizing it. This is how it goes down between you:

   a. He apologizes to you and says that he never meant to hurt your feelings. You apologize back. It's not all his fault, and you take some of the blame.

   b. You apologize to him, even though you both started it. You certainly feel better, but when he fails to respond in the same way, it's a little annoying.

   c. He tells you that everything that happened is totally his fault—he started it and he should take responsibility. You let him.

7. You're happy dating Brad, but then an ex-crush, Alex, comes into town. Alex texts you ahead of time and starts to do the flirty back-and-forth message thing we're all familiar with. You don't feel totally right about it because you're with Brad now. You:

   a. Tell Alex that you are in a relationship now. It's best to be honest before you dig yourself into a hole.

b. Keep texting the crush. You like Brad, but you've only been dating a few weeks. It's always good to have a backup plan.

c. Completely ignore the texts. If you don't respond, they'll go away.

THE RESULTS

1. a-1, b-2, c-3
2. a-2, b-1, c-3
3. a-3, b-1, c-2
4. a-1, b-3, c-2
5. a-1, b-2, c-3
6. a-2, b-3, c-1
7. a-2, b-1, c-3

WHAT YOUR SCORE MEANS

7–11 POINTS: HE IS DEFINITELY INTO YOU

Well, sweetie, you've definitely accomplished what you set out to do. He is into you, no doubt about it. Do you like him as much as he adores you, though? If you scored in this area, chances are you need to do a little more evaluating before you get into something serious with this guy.

12–17 POINTS: IT'S MUTUAL

Sweet glory, you both loooove each other. It's totally mutual between you two. Nothing to worry about.

18–21 Points: You Definitely Like Him

So, you like him, that much is certain. Don't jump in over your head, though. If you are doing everything right and he isn't responding as you expect him to, he may need a little more time to reach the same wavelength. Don't give it all away to a guy who needs more convincing, though. He should be doing some of the work too. And remember the Golden Rule! You believe in yourself, and if this guy doesn't, then it's probably time to ditch him for someone who would love to be on the same page as you.

AMAZINGLY COOL DATES

Thank you for your patience during that quiz. It was sort of like when you are gearing up for takeoff on an airplane: The flight attendant asks you to pay attention to the safety demonstration and you dutifully follow suit. Now that we've gotten all that jazz out of the way, we can start exploring the incredibly fun ways you can build the relationship you have with your sweetie into a marvelous one.

One way to do that? Spend quality time together by going on really great dates. This is a perfect opportunity to do something with your lovey that you've always wanted to do but have never tried. Lose those inhibitions, girl! Pick anything you want: It's bound to be fun if you're doing it together. It's really nice to spend quality time with the person you love, and doing something that encourages togetherness is what make "great dates" so fun.

I know that my faithful readers are of varying ages and incomes, so I'm going to divide up these amazingly cool dates based on their price ranges. I'll start off with the *free* dates (!!!), move into affordable ones, and end with a bang as we discuss all the things you can splurge on together. Personally, I find some of the free dates to be the most pleasurable. These dates focus on the experiences you have together rather than the dollar amount spent. And if you're doing something that costs absolutely nothing, you're bound to appreciate the thoughtfulness that went into it. It's actually harder than you think to spend nothing on a date (Try not buying the Diet Coke you want so badly!). Let's go!

FREE DATES

- **Video game challenge.** I'm sure your boyfriend loves video games and already owns some kind of game console. And you aren't too shabby yourself: Your days of Super Mario and Donkey Kong will surely come in handy when you challenge your sweetie to an all-out competition playing your favorite video game. Make sure to practice ahead of time, though! The winner gets a special (and free) treat from the loser, like a massage or maybe just some simple ego stroking.

- **Get up early, or stay up all night.** Do it one way or the other, but make sure to catch a sunrise with that special someone. Sunrises have a way of filling the room with soft pink light that a sunset cannot match. It's a romantic way to spend a quiet part of the day together. Make sure to set your alarm in case you lovebirds fall asleep during go time.
- **Get outdoors.** One of my favorite free dates is going on a long hike with my boyfriend. We take the dog, pack some water bottles and snacks, and head out. Pick a trail that you've never done before and enjoy.
- **Play with puppies.** Go to your local animal shelter with your BF and spend some time with all the animals in need of love. You're bound to have a fulfilling experience, and maybe you'll find a new friend to take home together!
- **The Big Give.** Give each other gifts based on stuff you find around the house. Each of you should pick five things that you know will have meaning for your sweetie. Opening your special presents will bring lots of laughs, will remind you of good times spent together, and is bound to be a good time. As an added bonus, do this gift exchange during a random time of the year rather than the holidays.
- **Scavenge away.** You remember going on scavenger

hunts at your friends' childhood birthday parties, right? So fun! This scavenger hunt is taken to a new level, however, because you aren't collecting *things*, you're collecting photos. Before you head out, make a list of all the places, people, or things you'll have to take photos with, and after you do it, print out all the pictures as mementos. I like to do this in a popular area with lots of people, parks, or shops. Come up with a theme for your photo hunt—like, you have to take pictures with ten people who are more than six feet four inches tall and wearing green T-shirts.

- **Learn something new.** You've always wanted to learn how to surf, play football, or drive stick shift. Your boyfriend has these skills, so ask him to teach you how. Make sure to listen closely and not crash his car.

- **Virtual date.** If you and your boyfriend can't get together, schedule a virtual date with each other. Download Skype or iChat, enable the video function, and have at it. Do whatever it is you wanted to do in person: Eat dinner together, talk about your day, whatever.

- **Play H-O-R-S-E.** We all played this competitive basketball game as kids. Now it's time to take it to the next level.

- **Hit the books.** We all have to get work done at some point, and what better way to study than with your cutie? Set some study hours together and hit the books. Help each other out by making quiz note cards. Good luck not getting too distracted!
- **Create a date list.** Make a list of all the things you want to do together. Set dates and stick to them!

AFFORDABLE DATES

- **Game night.** Game night with your boyfriend and a group of couples sounds cheesy in theory but is awesome in reality. Buy some classic games or dig them out of your closet, then team up and compete! Game night tip: Make sure to include a game of hide-and-seek. Finding hiding spots as a big kid is way tougher—and funnier—than you think.
- **Brunch and a matinee.** Breakfast out is far more affordable than dinner at a restaurant. A matinee movie is often half the price of a later flick. So spend the morning with your guy and do both together. It's fun to do something you both love but in a slightly different way.
- **At-home spa.** You love a great massage, and your boyfriend loves them too. Plan an at-home

spa day with your lovey by going to Bath & Body Works together and buying your favorite lotion. At home, give each other a massage you'll both never forget.

- **Watch the game.** Every town has a local team to support. Find the schedule for your favorite local baseball team, soccer club, or high school football game and enjoy the evening supporting them together. Take a blanket to share in the stands and snacks to munch on.

- **Rock out.** Go see a new band that is playing a free or near-free show at a local venue. They'll take all the new fans they can get, and you and your guy can enjoy dancing the night away together on the cheap.

- **Wash the car.** Be prepared for a water fight! Park both of your dirty rides on the street and wash them together until they are sparkling. For some extra fun bring along some water balloons and a squirt gun. He won't know what hit him.

- **The farmers' market.** Hitting up your local farmer's market for fresh flowers and veggies isn't only fun and healthy, it's cheap. Go together and plan a dinner or lunch on the fly based on what you buy. Point out your favorite flowers to him, and maybe he'll be sweet enough to pick them up for you. The farmers' market is a great way to experience that street-fair feel together every week.

- **Browse for books.** Go on a late-night date to your local bookstore. A lot of places have an in-store café, so enjoy a hot chocolate together. Browse for your next read—you could even pick out each other's books—and spend some quality time perusing the magazines.

EXTRAVAGANT DATES

- **Day trippin'.** Choose a fun destination a few hours away from home and make a day trip out of it. Leave early, stop for breakfast at a scenic restaurant, and arrive refreshed and ready to go. Pick something you'll both enjoy doing: a long hike at a big park, a day at an amazing aquarium, or skydiving in the desert. Take a camera with you and document the day together.
- **Throw a party.** There's no better way to have fun with your boyfriend than throwing a party together. Pick a time and a place, invite all your friends, and do the work together. Plan a menu, buy decorations, and enjoy each other's company all at the same time. Your friends will be impressed by your teamwork.
- **Foodie feast.** Make a reservation at the hot new

restaurant in town and show up dressed to the nines. Order a full meal: appetizers, salad, a main course, dessert, and drinks. Going all out has never tasted so good.

- **Theme park adventure.** Spending a day at a theme park with your boyfriend is a great way to let loose and have fun. Let out your inner kid and take goofy photos, play enough games to win a stuffed animal, and eat a greasy lunch. My favorite theme park is Disneyland, but if you can't make it to Orange County, California, there's bound to be a theme park or local carnival near you.

- **Cook together.** Take a cooking class together to learn how to make your favorite meal from a pro. Learn great knife skills, or tasks as basic as chopping lettuce. Your boyfriend loves it when you cook for him, and this is a fun way to incorporate him into the process. He'll love learning some new techniques, and it's guaranteed he'll surprise you with some home cooking of his own after you whip up treats with an advanced chef.

- **Limo date.** Let's be honest, the best part of high school dances is getting to ride around town in a huge limo. Re-create this fun by renting a car service for a night on the town with your boyfriend. What's even better is that you'll have the limo to yourselves, so a little backseat smoochfest is totally cool.

- **Ride high in a hot-air balloon.** Take to the skies with your sweetie in an awesome hot-air balloon. This adventure may require a little travel to get there, but it'll be worth it when you see the spectacular view. Take along some drinks and snacks for a picnic in the sky.

- **Make ice cream.** Buy an ice cream maker and get to work churning out your boyfriend's favorite treat at home. It's a great way to spend a little quality dessert time together in your pj's. Make more than one flavor for an extra-delicious evening of creamy delights.

- **Hit the driving range.** Get your competitive spirit going with a trip to the driving range with your boyfriend. Even if you don't know how to swing a club, the driving range is a stress-free place to learn the basics. Make a bet with your boyfriend as to whose ball will go the farthest. The driving range takes the putt-putt course date to a whole new level of fun.

- **Score tickets to the game.** Score your sweetie tickets to the big game and encourage him to go with a friend. Even though you're staying home, he will think it's the coolest, most awesome thing you've ever done for him. He is bound to pay you back in kind.

- **Prepare sushi.** We all love, love, love sushi, and making it at home is fun and super rewarding. Show off your amazing cooking skills by whipping up some basic rolls for your hottie. Make sure to purchase sushi-grade fish from a reputable store and to sharpen your knives. Sticky rice is key, as is a bamboo mat to roll your dinner into something special. He will be superimpressed.

RECIPES FOR LOVE

Food is an important element in a relationship. It may not seem like it, but a lot of relationship activities revolve around eating. Think about it. Your first date is probably at a restaurant. Your first Thanksgiving together is all about a turkey. The first meal you cook for him or he cooks for you? Hello, milestone!

Now, this cooking section is not straight out of the 1950s, telling you to get your butt into the kitchen and stay there! No, no. It's about the magic of food, about how wonderfully fun it is to cook it, and about the joy of eating it!

So, why cook for your boyfriend?

- When you cook for your special someone, you're doing something nice for him.
- Eating together at home is something you will both look forward to. It lets you appreciate each other over a delicious dinner.
- Eating at home will keep you healthy, because you choose how much butter and everything else goes into the dish.
- Eating at home is cheaper than eating out. Save that extra money for a special date on a rainy day.
- Whenever he eats a dish out that you've also cooked for him, he will think of you. ☺

GETTING STARTED

Cooking, especially when you're a beginner, can be stressful. For me, though, it's the total opposite. Cooking is like my personal meditation/yoga/spa session all at once. The smell of cooking onions, the feel of the sharp knife in my hand— it's enough to put me into a subliminal trance for the rest of the day.

My wildest hope and dream is to get you to that Julia Child–esque place as well, and trust me, it's easier than you think. Before you plan a divine feast for your guy, though, make sure to read through your recipe thoroughly and understand how to do every step. If you don't understand a process, Google it! Nothing is worse than stressing out over a special meal during the prep. Pick a recipe that you and he both love and that you know you can execute.

The following recipes are ones I absolutely love to make and eat, and they're all boyfriend tested and approved. Quite a few of them are from my mom, the wonderful woman who has taught me how to cook over the past few years. She learned how to create everything from cakes to outrageously tasty steaks when she started dating my dad. Everyone has to start from square one in the kitchen, though, and these recipes here are simple and tasty. Good luck and happy cooking, my friends.

Lo's Gruyère Frittata

(Serves 4)

Ingredients:

8 EGG WHITES (OR 6 WHOLE EGGS,
IF YOU PREFER TO INCLUDE THE YOLKS)

¾ C. WATER

½ C. GRUYÈRE

1 C. CUBED BUTTERNUT SQUASH

1 C. RAW SPINACH

1 C. ASPARAGUS, CUT INTO 1-INCH PIECES

SALT AND PEPPER TO TASTE

1 T. OLIVE OIL

COOKING SPRAY

Steps:

1. Preheat your oven to 350 degrees.
2. Put raw, cubed butternut squash into a Ziploc bag and microwave for 5–7 minutes until cooked through. You'll know it's done when a piece is easily pierced by a fork.
3. While the squash is cooking, heat up the olive oil in a pan at medium heat. Add the asparagus to the pan and salt and pepper to taste. Cook until almost tender. Throw the cooked squash in for a minute at the end to brown the pieces.

4. Put the cooked squash and asparagus into a large bowl along with the raw spinach. Add the water and egg whites to the veggies. Add almost all the cheese. Mix until the veggies are thoroughly coated. Add salt and pepper, then pour the egg mixture into a 9-inch cake pan that has been coated with cooking spray. Top the mixture with the remaining cheese.

5. Bake for 30 minutes or until the liquid becomes a fluffy solid and enjoy!

Lo's Spicy Breakfast Burritos

(Serves 2)

Ingredients:

4 EGG WHITES

4 T. ROASTED TOMATO SALSA (MEDIUM HEAT)

¼ LB. GROUND TURKEY

10 CHERRY TOMATOES, CUT IN HALF

⅛ C. GRATED CHEDDAR CHEESE

2 LARGE TORTILLAS

SALT AND PEPPER TO TASTE

COOKING SPRAY

Steps:

1. Coat your frying pan with cooking spray and heat up over medium heat. Add ¼ lb. of ground turkey and the salsa to the pan. Add the cherry tomatoes, cut sides facing down. Cook the turkey thoroughly.

2. Lower the heat and add the egg whites to the pan, as well as salt and pepper to taste. Scramble the eggs as they become mixed in with the turkey, salsa, and tomatoes.

3. Divide the egg mixture into two portions and place on tortillas. Carefully roll the filled tortillas to create the burritos. Top the eggs with a bit of cheese and enjoy!

Mom's Tortilla Soup

Ingredients:

1 ½ C. SLICED RED ONION

2 GARLIC CLOVES, MINCED

1 T. OLIVE OIL

1 T. CHILI POWDER

1 T. CUMIN

1 SMALL CAN OF RO*TEL TOMATOES AND CHILIES

6 C. CHICKEN BROTH

1 C. CORN

1 14-OZ. CAN OF MEXICAN-STYLE DICED TOMATOES

1 ½ C. CUBED CHICKEN (BUY A PREROASTED CHICKEN AND CUT THE CHICKEN OFF THE BONE AND INTO PIECES)

5 CORN TORTILLAS CUT INTO STRIPS (YOU DECIDE HOW BIG OR SMALL)

LIMES

CILANTRO

1 AVOCADO, CHOPPED

SALT AND PEPPER TO TASTE

Steps:

1. In a large pot (try for enameled cast iron, like a big dutch oven), sauté the onion and garlic in oil over medium-low heat. Be careful not to burn the garlic. If you do, start over.

2. Add the chili powder and cumin and cook for 30 seconds more.

3. Add the tomatoes and chilies, chicken broth, corn, and diced tomatoes. Season with salt and pepper.

4. Bring to a boil, then reduce the heat.

5. Add the chicken and let the mixture simmer over low heat for 10 minutes.

6. Garnish with tortillas, lime, cilantro, and avocado and enjoy!

Fumi Salad

Ingredients:

SALAD:

1 HEAD OF PURPLE CABBAGE, CHOPPED

8 CHOPPED GREEN ONIONS

8 T. SLIVERED ALMONDS, BROWNED

8 T. SESAME SEEDS, BROWNED

2 PACKAGES OF *UNCOOKED* TOP RAMEN NOODLES,
BROKEN INTO PIECES

DRESSING:

4 T. SUGAR

1 C. OLIVE OIL

1 T. PEPPER

2 T. SALT

6 T. RICE VINEGAR

Steps:

1. Wash and dry chopped cabbage. Combine all the salad ingredients in a large bowl.

2. Combine all the ingredients for the dressing and refrigerate the mixture until the salad is ready.

3. Combine the dressing and salad and serve immediately.

Lo's Goat Cheese Pasta
with Asparagus and Lemon

Ingredients:

1 LB. WHOLE WHEAT PASTA,

PREFERABLY BOW TIES OR PENNE

15 SPEARS OF ASPARAGUS, CUT INTO 1-INCH PIECES

JUICE FROM HALF A LEMON

ZEST FROM 1 LEMON

½ C. BOILING WATER, FROM PASTA

5 T. GOAT CHEESE

OLIVE OIL

SALT AND PEPPER

Steps:

1. In your serving bowl, combine the juice from half a lemon, the lemon zest, 1 t. salt, and 1 t. pepper.

2. Following the instructions on the package, cook the pasta until tender.

3. While you are cooking the pasta, sauté the chopped asparagus in a few tablespoons of olive oil in a pan over medium heat, until tender. Season the veggies with salt and pepper.

4. When the pasta finishes cooking, reserve ½ c. of the cooking water, then drain the pasta and transfer to the serving bowl.

5. Add the goat cheese, asparagus, and reserved cooking water to the serving bowl immediately.

6. Toss the mixture until the goat cheese melts into a creamy sauce over the pasta.

7. Taste before serving. This dish is best served with a lot of lemon, so add a little more juice if the flavor needs heightening.

Mom's Roasted Garlic Chicken

Ingredients:

1 ROASTING CHICKEN, WASHED AND DRIED

7 BULBS OF RAW GARLIC

2 T. OLIVE OIL

2 T. BUTTER, SOFTENED

2 T. SALT

1 T. PEPPER

Steps:

1. Preheat oven to 450 degrees. Wash the whole chicken, inside and out, in cool water. Remove the giblets from the interior of the bird. Dry the chicken thoroughly.

2. Season the interior and exterior of the bird with salt and pepper. Take all the cloves from one of the bulbs and place them inside the chicken.

3. Drizzle the olive oil over the chicken until its evenly coated. Massage the soft butter over the outside of the chicken and under the layer of skin.

4. Set the chicken in a large baking dish with low sides, and put into the 450-degree oven.

5. After 30 minutes, lower the temperature to 350 degrees and cook for another 15 minutes.

6. During this time, take the 6 remaining bulbs of garlic

and, keeping the bulbs intact, cut off the tops of each so each raw clove is slightly exposed. After the chicken has cooked for 15 minutes at 350 degrees, add the bulbs, cut sides down, to the baking dish. Be sure to place the bulbs in an area of the dish with liquid in it.

7. Cook the chicken for 45 more minutes at 350 degrees. When the juices of the chicken run clear, remove it from the oven and let it sit for 10 minutes.

8. Cut the chicken into pieces and use the cooked garlic bulbs as a sort of creamy spread. To do this, squeeze the cooked cloves out of the bulb and mash them across each piece of chicken. Enjoy!

Maura's Calzones

Ingredients:

1 STORE-BOUGHT PIZZA DOUGH

FLOUR

TOMATO-BASED PIZZA SAUCE

CHEDDAR CHEESE

VEGGIES OF YOUR CHOOSING, PRECOOKED

COOKING SPRAY

Steps:

1. Preheat oven to 400 degrees.
2. Cut or tear the pizza dough into fist-size pieces and roll each piece out on a flour-covered surface.
3. Top each piece of dough with pizza sauce, then with precooked veggies and cheese. Make sure not to add too many toppings, and don't let them get too close to the edge of the dough.
4. Fold dough in half to create a calzone shape. Make sure the edges of the dough are sealed tightly together.
5. Place the calzones on a baking sheet prepped with cooking spray. Bake for 15 minutes or until the dough is cooked through.

Spinach Salad

Ingredients:

1 BAG OF PREWASHED SPINACH

10 STRIPS OF BACON

½ RED ONION, CHOPPED

2 ANJOU PEARS, CHOPPED

3 HARD-BOILED EGGS, CHOPPED

½ C. CRUMBLED BLUE CHEESE

3 T. HONEY DIJON POPPY DRESSING

Steps:

1. Pan-fry bacon until crispy (or microwave using the package directions, if pressed for time). Let the bacon cool, then crumble it and set it aside.

2. Chop onion, pears, and eggs and place in a large bowl with spinach, crumbled bacon, and blue cheese.

3. Toss salad with poppy dressing and eat up!

Mom's Homemade Macaroni and Cheese

Ingredients:

1 LB. ELBOW MACARONI

2 CUPS LOWFAT MILK

3 CUPS SHARP CHEDDAR CHEESE, GRATED

¾ C. BREAD CRUMBS

3 T. BUTTER

½ C. COOKED HAM PIECES, CHOPPED

2 EGGS, BEATEN

1 T. CHICKEN BOUILLON

⅛ T. NUTMEG

⅛ T. PEPPER

¼ T. SALT

Steps:

1. Preheat your oven to 350 degrees.
2. Cook the macaroni in boiling water until tender. Strain and pour into a large casserole dish or dutch oven.
3. Melt butter in a frying pan over medium heat and cook the ham until the edges of each piece are crunchy.
4. Add the ham, milk, eggs, cheese, bouillon, and spices to the macaroni. Stir together and top with bread crumbs.
5. Bake for 30 minutes, uncovered. If you like the top of your mac and cheese to be crunchy, broil at the end of the 30 minutes, for 1 to 2 minutes. Enjoy!

Mom's Best Chicken Fettuccini

Ingredients:

2 CUPS CHICKEN, COOKED AND CUBED

1 CUP SLICED MUSHROOMS

⅓ STICK OF BUTTER

1 ½ C. PARMESAN CHEESE

1 LB. OF WHOLE WHEAT FETTUCCINI

SAUCE:

3 T. BUTTER

3 T. FLOUR

2 C. CHICKEN BROTH

1 T. CHICKEN BOUILLON

1 C. CREAM, OR ¾ C. CREAM COMBINED WITH ¼ C. HALF-AND-HALF

3 T. COOKING SHERRY (IF YOU'RE 21-PLUS YEARS OLD)

1 T. SALT

½ T. PEPPER

Steps:

1. Sauté mushrooms in butter until browned. Remove mushrooms and then cook chicken in the same pan. Set aside.
2. Cook the noodles until tender and set aside.
3. To make the cream sauce, you will need to make a roux. To do this, melt butter in a medium-size pan over medium heat, then add flour. Stir constantly for a minute or two. Add the broth, chicken bouillon, cream, sherry,

and seasonings. Stir over medium-low heat until creamy but still very pourable. This entire process will take only a few minutes. Don't let the sauce sit for too long or it may become too thick. If it does, add more milk until the desired consistency is achieved.

4. Place the noodles, mushrooms, and chicken in a casserole dish. Pour the sauce over the ingredients and toss until combined thoroughly. Sprinkle the top with cheese and bake in a 350-degree oven for 15 minutes, or a bit longer if you prepared it in advance and it's coming out of the refrigerator. *Yum.*

Muddy Buddies

My family often delivers Muddy Buddies to our
neighbors during the holidays as a small treat.

Ingredients:

9 C. CHEX CEREAL (NOT WHEAT FLAVOR)

1 C. CHOCOLATE CHIPS

½ C. PEANUT BUTTER

¼ C. BUTTER

¼ T. VANILLA

12 OZ. PEANUTS

1 ½ C. POWDERED SUGAR

Steps:

1. Put dry cereal in a large bowl or pan.
2. Melt chocolate, peanut butter, and butter for 1 minute in the microwave. Stir, and cook 1 minute more until smooth. Add the vanilla.
3. Handling the bowl or pan very carefully, since it will be hot, pour the chocolate mix on top of the cereal. Mix gently, trying not to break the pieces of cereal.
4. Put the cereal in a large trash bag (weird, I know) and add the peanuts and powdered sugar. Close the bag and shake it until every piece is covered in sugary goodness.
5. Pour the Muddy Buddies onto wax paper to dry. Enjoy!

Lemon Bars

Ingredients:

CRUST:

2 C. FLOUR

1 C. SOFT BUTTER

½ C. POWDERED SUGAR

FILLING:

4 EGGS

1 ¾ C. SUGAR

DASH OF SALT

5 T. OR MORE LEMON JUICE

1 T. BAKING POWDER

¼ C. FLOUR

Steps:

1. Preheat your oven to 350 degrees.
2. Mix ingredients for crust in food processor or mixer and press into a 9 x 13-inch glass dish.
3. Bake for 20 minutes.
4. Meanwhile, mix together eggs, sugar, salt, and lemon juice. Fold the flour and baking powder into the wet ingredients.
5. Pour the mix onto the hot crust and bake for at least 30 minutes.
6. Once the lemon bars come out of the oven, sprinkle with powdered sugar and let cool to completely solidify.

THE STUFF HE'LL LOVE TO DO FOR YOU

You love your boyfriend and you love going out of your way to do special things for him. Ask your sexy self *why* you do all of these nice things and you'll answer that you do them because he is totally worth it. The amazing thing about a great relationship is that the feelings you have for him are mutual between you. Just like you do nice things for him, he wants to do really satisfying things for you too. He loves you back, he trusts you, and he wants you to feel just as exceptional as you make him feel every single day.

You've become the person who understands him without judgment, and he appreciates this about you. As a result, he wants to take care of the lady who loves him unequivocally.

While you enjoy cooking him dinner and don't mind picking up his dry cleaning, he may show his love for you in other ways—coming home with fresh flowers for you or sending you to the spa for the day. He loves spending time with you after a long day full of work or friends, because your presence relaxes him. No matter what happened that day, being with you makes it all okay.

Frequently, the other things he does for you are more unexpected but perhaps even more important. He makes it a point to join in on the stuff you already like to do, even if it's girly or he hates it. Because these things are *already* a part of your life, you may not notice that his participation in them indicates his love for *you*, rather than for whatever activity it is.

For example, you've always loved *Grey's Anatomy*, but it's definitely not his favorite show. He is more of a *SportsCenter* guy, but he joins you on the couch every Thursday without fail . . . because he loves you.

Even though he is crazy busy during the day, he e-mails you every day at one o'clock since he knows you always check your messages at lunchtime . . . because he loves you.

Your schedule requires you to wake up thirty minutes before he does every day, but he chooses to get up with you anyway. He kisses you good-bye every single morning . . . because he loves you.

For him, regularly doing small things for you is his way of showing how much he values you and your relationship. Of course, when he does something special out of the blue it's great, but be sure to value the little ways he shows you his love every day. He does them because you deserve it and he wants to give back to you just as much as you give to him.

WHY QUIRKS IRK

We've all been there before: You and your guy have been together for four-ish months and everything is really comfortable between you. But feeling more comfortable with your special someone can mean you start to notice insignificant things about this person that maybe, just maybe, drive you absolutely nuts. You all know what I'm talking about. There is no way around this part of a relationship. You love this person, but the way he does this or how he says that can really start to bug you.

It's a dangerous moment for any partnership. And trust me, you're not the only one feeling a teensy bit antsy. Maybe he doesn't like how often you pick at your nails or that you always leave all the lights on at your house (Seriously, you should stop: it's time to get serious about patching up our environment).

Whatever it is, you both consider small things about each other to be a little annoying.

Take your lovely author, for example. In high school, month four of a relationship was about the time I broke things off. Stuff about my guy would just start to bug me. I'd notice a quirk and focus on it so much that I would allow something insignificant to completely ruin a potentially great relationship. I remember breaking up with one guy because he wore shorts with Sperry Top-Siders far too often. I mean, who am I? Seriously? I was a jerk sometimes, let's be real.

It was a real problem for me, but it's one that I've made strides in overcoming thanks to a blunt wake-up call from my current, amazing boyfriend. He taught me that if you love somebody, it's necessary to love them completely. Stop loving your guy Monday through Friday but saying forget it when he watches football games nonstop on the weekends. It's a seven-day a week commitment.

The way he lives his life, as long as it doesn't affect your well-being, is something that at around the fourth-month mark you must learn to not concern yourself with. Why? For one, you'll go crazy if you focus continually on something that truly has *zero* effect on you. In addition, you're his girlfriend, not his mommy. He'll fold his shirts when he wants to. If you start to poke at his personal stuff, he will resent you for it. Would you want him to criticize the way you've always done things in return? Nope. So forget it.

I'll repeat: For your own sanity and the health of your relationship, it's time to grow up and get over whatever little thing it is that bothers you about him. It's far easier and far more loving to *just let it go* than to attack him for always wearing a jersey on game day. We all have our quirks. Whether you fancy them or not is not going to change them. Whether or not you keep your opinions to yourself *will*, however, have an effect on your relationship.

With the help of this really awesome guidebook, you've come to understand that you are perfect the way you are—but you still have quirks, and he does too! It's just a fact of life. So, once you land that hottie from chem lab, you start to get to know him, but for a relationship to blossom, you must give him just as much respect as he gives you. So, it is absolutely not worth it to whip yourself into a frenzy over something your boyfriend does that bugs you. It's just his way—who he is. He loves *you*, quirks and all, and it's time you loved *him* for all of his somewhat interesting habits.

Can you even imagine having a serious conversation with your boyfriend about something he does that does not affect you yet drives you up the wall? It would be an incredibly hurtful and insensitive conversation. Just like you would say to yourself, "Seriously?" if your guy attacked something inconsequential you do, he would feel the exact same way if you did that to him.

So, is there a way to have an appropriate conversation

about one of your boyfriend's quirks? Only—I repeat, only—if what he is doing is being done *to you*. If you are on the receiving end of some sort of behavior that you find annoying or weird, speak up, but with caution. The best way to go about doing this is by casually asking your boyfriend if you could talk briefly about something that's been bugging you. He will definitely say yes, and you must follow through once you start the conversation. Explain to him gently that x, y, or z has a negative effect on you. In this explanation you must make clear *why* it's an issue. Simply stating what bugs you will not get you anywhere, and will feel like outright criticism. He needs to understand where you are coming from and why. Be sure to stay calm, be polite, and love on him immediately afterward. Change the subject once it's discussed, highlight something you love about him, or give him a kiss on the cheek.

In these kinds of scenarios, boyfriends frequently have no idea that what they are doing to you drives you up the wall. Perhaps your boyfriend's last girlfriend loved to be snuggled constantly but you do not. He is just doing what he thinks is right. Explaining yourself and your situation takes the personal bite out of it and turns something that annoys you into a nonissue.

All in all, just remember all the amazing things about your sweetie when a little nothing creeps up out of nowhere. Be the bigger, better, more evolved girl I know you are: Treat him and his ways with the same respect you expect from him. Do this, and your relationship with your sweetie is guaranteed to last far longer than the dangerous irk stage. Trust me. I have some experience.

THINGS TO WORK ON TOGETHER

Ladies, maintaining a relationship requires love and attention, despite how perfect you two may be for each other. There are things beyond fun dates and delicious homemade meals, though, that keep a blossoming relationship continually blooming. It's the everyday stuff, the kinds of things you learned in your friendships as a kid, that will continue to strengthen your bond with your stud muffin of a boyfriend.

If you don't already practice the following five togetherness tips, make sure to work them into your relationship. Utilizing these five togetherness tips will modify the kind of girl you are—but in a good way. Incorporating these changes into your life doesn't mean I'm going back on my Golden

Rule. These tips help you develop into a more desirable Golden Girl: a well-rounded and learned lady with a hottie, hot, hot boyfriend.

NUMBER ONE: COMMUNICATE

Communicating with your boyfriend is key. The more mature you become, the easier it is to stand up for yourself. Who knows where this newfound confidence comes from as you start to grow up, but it's definitely there. Not that you'll need to stick up for yourself with your boyfriend, but it's this confidence that will teach you how to communicate efficiently with him. Frequently, when you have to have a "talk," it's a slightly uncomfortable situation. Get over being uncomfortable for three seconds, hit the ground running, and get whatever it is that's bugging you off your chest. Communicating well also creates a positive day-to-day environment free of confusion and misinterpretation. Start talkin'!

NUMBER TWO: SAY YOU'RE SORRY

Saying sorry—it's something we are taught to do as children. Being able to apologize to your partner if you do something icky is one of the key togetherness tips for any positive relationship. If you can't say you're sorry, you'll run into serious issues. A person who is able to take a little heat and apologize is far more evolved, not to mention admirable, than the immature amoeba who keeps all their guilt inside.

NUMBER THREE: LAUGH IT OFF

Just like being able to say you are sorry is important, being able to laugh it off is essential. Why? Not every little thing that goes wrong is the end of the world. Just because you accidentally tooted in front of your boyfriend when you got home from dinner doesn't mean he's going to break up with you. Laugh it off. You wont be exiled to a deserted desert island because a little gas got in the way. Anyway, most boys like farts.

NUMBER FOUR: LOVE EACH OTHER

That's right, loving each other is one of the five togetherness tips. This one seems obvious, but a hug and a kiss here and there make a big difference! If you and your sweetie get into a habit of loving on each other frequently, you'll be happier and healthier. Instead of just expressing your love through your emotions, you physical actions will help to *show* the love between you too.

NUMBER FIVE: SPEND TIME TOGETHER

Not every second you spend together needs to be on a wonderful date or out-of-this-world adventure. Sometimes the best times you spend together are snuggling up on the couch with a good movie. Make a little time for your sweetie every single day. Whether you see him or you just chat on the phone, a little boyfriend time is necessary every single day.

PART 5

ALL THE
OTHER STUFF

SO, WHAT ABOUT ALL THE OTHER STUFF? WAIT . . . WHAT OTHER stuff is there? You now know how to single out all the loser guys out there, you get why they make you feel sucky, and you understand how to overcome their negative energy and believe in yourself. You've picked a perfect ten, and now he is your boyfriend! I've covered it all. Seriously, what else is there?

Okay. Fiiiiiine. I won't pretend for another paragraph that there isn't anything else to relationships.

All the other stuff. The stuff that nobody really likes to face: the sometimes serious bumps in the relationship road. Yes, unfortunately it's true that sometimes, once in a blue moon, every so often every other decade, you may have what I call a *breakup* on your hands.

In the actual breaking-up moment, the dissolving of what could have been a perfect partnership (in fantasyland) does hurt. But let's face the facts: A breakup is a breakup for a reason. The relationship that's being torn to pieces is not working. It's as simple as that. And because it's considered standard human behavior to discuss an official *end* to a relationship instead of walking away one day, never to speak again, the actual moment of breaking up is inevitable but necessary.

Instead of dreading breakups like they symbolize the end of the world, let's approach them in a new way. The guy you're saying "peace" to is simply a mismatched piece in your love puzzle. That's right, girls, I'm bringing the puzzle analogy back to the table. I'm serious, though. You're breaking up with, or being broken up with a mismatched puzzle piece. *Your* puzzle piece is a constant, sexy, unwavering piece of configured cardboard, and his was just way too sharp on one side. He didn't fit with you—end of story.

When you simplify a breakup into something as easily explainable as mismatched puzzle pieces, it allows you to understand that while you are hurting, the end of your relationship is not the end of the world. Instead, it's a new beginning.

Sure, you're single all of a sudden. But, hello! You're single! That means instead of spending night after night on the couch with your ex-loser doing the same old thing, you get to put on your hottest outfit, pretty yourself up, and feel absolutely fantabulous whenever, wherever, and with whomever. You are officially free. That's a pretty great feeling, one that is sure to make up for whatever nastiness you encountered when it ended with your ex.

More than anything, breaking up is really about picking yourself back up again. You go into a breakup understanding that you're about to be on your own for a while but that singledom is something to enjoy rather than wallow in. You get to start over again with a better guy. You get to have a better relationship than the one you just left. A breakup allows you to experience the types of relationships that you've always desired and that really do exist.

QUIZ: FLING VS. RELATIONSHIP

This quiz will reveal whether what you're experiencing has relationship potential or is merely a fling. Flings are great: They can be fun, extremely fulfilling, and a nice way to learn about another person. A fling is not a relationship, however. If you're flinging it but you desire more, it's quite an undertaking to change what you currently have into something more serious. Why? Because you've approached it in a laid-back way from the beginning. It's a fling because at some point you gave off signs that you're serious about having fun, but not much more.

And if a fling is all you're looking for, that's fabulous.

Enjoy yourself and learn from this new "friend." If you want a relationship, however, how you score on this quiz will be a good indicator of whether what you're experiencing is serious or not. Let's get to it.

1. You and the cute guy you've been hanging out with a lot haven't talked in a few days. Nothing happened, really, you just sort of stopped communicating. Maybe he is busy or something, but maybe not. You want to keep seeing him but reaching out after a few days of very little chatting seems sort of awkward. When you do shoot him a text saying, "Hey! Where have you been the past zillion years?" he responds like this:

    a. "Babe. Been thinking about you. Sorry I've been MIA the past little while. Let's get together after work tomorrow night. Say, 7:00 p.m., your place, cool?"

    b. "Right where I've always been! Me and the boys are going snowboarding for a few days. Where have you been?"

2. You know that something is up with Brad. You don't know if it's something you did a few days ago that's bothering him or if it's a different issue. You're pretty sure if you say nothing then whatever it is that's wrong will go away on its own. On the other hand, it makes

more sense to ask him what's up so you can move beyond it. You:

    a.   Continue to ignore what's up.

    b.   Ask him what's going on.

3. You know the gossip that sometimes occurs when two people start dating. You dislike it, because the subject matter frequently revolves around how the guy is dating this new girl but is still seeing girl *x, y,* or *z* on the side. So, you apply this to your new relationship and ask yourself if you still hear any of this dreaded chatter after a few weeks. The answer is:

    a.   Yes (*ick*).

    b.   No (*phew*).

4. You love to spend time with your new guy. It's always really, really fun. You make each other laugh and haven't gotten in any fights yet. What kinds of things do you do together?

    a.   A combo of nights at home, dinners out, and the occasional social gathering.

    b.   Lots of parties with friends, days at the beach with your crew, and some late-night TV time.

5. You've been dating Stephen for a month or two now. It's going pretty well, some dates here and there, a

million hour-long phone calls, and he's even met your sister. Out of nowhere, you two get into your first fight. It's sort of a nasty one because it's about his ex-girlfriend. After a decent amount of yelling at each other, you leave. You're frustrated and a little bit embarrassed because it probably seems like you're totally jealous of his ex, which you're not. After you cool down, you:

    a.   Talk it out with him.

    b.   Are too embarrassed to bring it up again, so you don't.

6. When you and Tripp first started to hang out, was it serious or casual? A better way to clarify this is to ask yourself, did you immediately start going on dates, or did you simply spend casual time together with friends, at parties, etc.?

    a.   Start hanging through dating.

    b.   Started hanging out in a pretty casual way.

7. It's your third month together. You are starting to feel like it's serious between you, and you'd like to make it official. When you broach the subject of being his girlfriend, he:

    a.   Laughs it off.

    b.   Makes it official!

THE RESULTS

1. a-1, b-2
2. a-2, b-1
3. a-2, b-1
4. a-1, b-2
5. a-1, b-2
6. a-1, b-2
7. a-2, b-1

WHAT YOUR SCORE MEANS

7–10 POINTS: IT'S A RELATIONSHIP!

Congratulations, sweetness. The guy you're dating is a keeper, and he is giving you the signs that indicate as much. He takes you on real dates, he spends quality time with you, and he is an open communicator. He listens to what you have to say, and if you get into an argument, there is always an amicable way to solve the problem. He is just as serious about having a relationship with you as you are with him. Celebrate: It's a true-life, flesh-and-blood relationship!

11–14 POINTS: IT'S A FLING

Maybe all you want is a fling, maybe not. The biggest difference between a fling and a relationship is how much the two people involved care for each other. If you want a fling, you want to have fun with someone you won't mind leaving down the line. You want it to be easy, and you avoid all the relationship stuff, like figuring out how to have a serious conversation. If you find yourself having a fling *but wanting a relationship*, chances are you're not following the Golden Rule. You're not putting the cool, calm, and collected girl you are out there. If you're constantly texting him, freaked out about whether he'll call you or not, or just plain stressed over him, it's likely you're coming off a little wackier than you truly are. Don't be that girl. Take a step back. The retreat will let the guy know something's up, and it's a good time to reapproach what you're doing in a more confident way or to have a conversation about getting more serious.

BREAKING UP

WHEN TO CALL IT OFF

You're living in the real world, not Candy Land, sugarpie, and sometimes stuff happens. Every once in a while you have to call it off . . . or he does. So, when should *you* call it off?

- **You have a gut feeling.** Your body does not lie to you. Frequently, that gut feeling really does signal that something is amiss. Don't always assume that the bad gut feeling you're having is precisely indicative of what you *think* it is; it could be speaking to you about something else you don't even see. Whatever the cause, a gut feeling is something to pay attention to. If it's strong enough, figure out what's causing it. If it's bad, call it off.

- **You are frequently unhappy.** Being unhappy in your relationship is standard every once in a while: Maybe your day didn't go your way or you and your man got into a little fight. Whatever! *But*, when you are unhappy in your relationship more often than you are happy with it, it's time to call it off. For me, when I'm crying in the shower more than twice a week over my boyfriend, it's about that time. When you're crying, pinpoint the reasons you are down, and work harder to make changes the next time around.

- **You make all the effort.** If you are making all the effort in your relationship, address the issue and ask for a change. If he doesn't start participating more often and you still feel like you're choosing all the dates, always asking about *his* day, and apologizing first in fights, call it off. Sounds to me like he doesn't care very much about making it work, and you are far more valuable than that.

HOW TO CALL IT OFF

First and foremost, if you are going to break up with someone, understand that you *must* go into the situation calm but ready. Chances are good that your new ex will be more than a little upset, as well as a bit embarrassed. You are about to put this person in an exceptionally vulnerable position, so be the kind, compassionate girl I know you are. Going overboard, rubbing it in, or being downright mean is completely uncalled for in a situation like this, and it's best to keep your head held high, no matter what you feel. In addition, if you make a breakup messy, you're bound to have additional nasty encounters with him in the future. Leaving bad blood makes people feel as though they'd like another shot at their newfound opponent, so it's best to remain calm and make a clean break from whomever this sad soul is.

That being said, let's get into it. First let's discuss the few-and-far-between moments you are allowed to break up with somebody over the phone or via e-mail (and this is *still* a sucker move). You may end it with a guy via technology if you are afraid of what his reaction may be. If you fear for your safety, use that cell phone, girl! In addition, sometimes it gets so bad with a guy that he literally will not give you a chance to see him, despite your many invitations to coffee. If he won't see you, allow your Gmail to let him have it. Be sure to include the explanation that because he won't see you, this is your only option.

If you've gone on one date, pick up the phone and let him know you'd rather be just friends. And even if you've been together longer than that and you just can't take it anymore, just do it. It may make you look like you pulled a cop-out move (you did), but in some cases your sanity is more important than a polite, face-to-face conversation.

Apart from these circumstances, the face-to-face breakup is key to leaving a relationship responsibly. Start the conversation by letting your future ex know what's up, but quickly move into the qualities you admire about him. Once you stroke his ego for a bit, discuss a concrete reason why you are calling it quits. This is not the time to be wishy-washy. Honesty is necessary and appreciated. Keep your honesty in check, though. No reason to go over the top.

Discuss when you started to feel differently about the relationship, not *him*. It's much kinder to discuss "the end" in terms of your relationship rather than in terms of what he specifically did wrong. It's far less personal that way. So, why did this happen to "our" relationship? How did you try to work through these feelings about *the relationship*? Answering these questions shows your responsible, thoughtful, and reasonable side. Answering these questions will help him to understand where and why it went wrong.

Finally, tell him you are sorry that your relationship has to end. It's never pretty to be on the receiving end of a breakup, and getting that sincere apology makes it a smidge easier if the initiating party takes some of the blame. Even if you do feel like it's all his fault when you end it, an apology to him will go a long way.

All in all, it's important to be straightforward and honest with the guy you're about to ditch. Keep your cool, remember your manners, and understand that he is most likely hurting more than you are. I know you can go through a breakup like the stud you really are. Prove to yourself and to him that you are worthy of such praise. If you do, it's quite possible that your ex will have nice things to say about you even after it's over.

WHEN HE CALLS IT OFF

Grrrr. It sucks to be on the receiving end of the breakup. Why? Because it leads you to believe that *you* did something to cause it. More often than not, this is not the case, even though it most always feels this way. Put it this way: You are you, and people choose to react to you, this force, this constant, however *they* want to. A change in their feelings is simply an indicator of their *reaction* to you, not a reflection of you.

Don't quite get it? Think again about how your puzzle piece is shaped. It's unique, and you are unable to change that, so you embrace it. Now think about all those other puzzle pieces around you. If you try to match one up with your constant, unchanging shape and that piece doesn't fit, that piece will deflect away from yours however *it* chooses to. You don't have *any control* over which way it goes afterward or why. Their puzzle piece is simply reacting to yours. In other words, the reaction someone has when they come into contact with you is not your responsibility. Your piece does not reach back out and try to fit with a piece that's already been tried with yours, because that would be changing who you are for another person.

To put this theory into practice, get out a puzzle and pick one piece that represents you. Tape it to the table. Have your mom pick up five random pieces and try to fit them against your piece. None of them fit? Okay, that's fine. Don't push it just so that one does. You are the best version of you when you are strong enough to understand that you don't have to cram or force your own piece against an ill-fitting one. Your perfect match is out there, and it's completely not worth it to compromise who you are for the wrong person. So, if you are being broken up with, remember that you are your own perfectly shaped puzzle piece. However this other pre-determined (and unchanging) shaped piece (the guy) is reacting to you is *not* within the realm of your control. He may have reacted to your piece in a way you don't like, but because you don't have a choice, an opportunity to affect his inevitable reaction, it cannot be your fault.

If you change yourself for another person, or for a relationship to work, it will lead you to believe that it is your fault if a breakup happens. You'll think that because you changed before, you should have been able to change again to fix how he felt. Thinking you can control another person's feelings by manipulating the person you appear to be is not indicative of a properly functioning relationship.

If you think going against how you really feel about something to fit into another person's relationship ideal will give you some kind of magic boy power you didn't have before, you are wrong. If you don't like that he texts other girls all hours of the day but you let him do it so that he stays with you, you are mis-representing how you really feel. He takes you to be a different person from the one you truly are. And your modification will be the reason your relationship comes to an end. Trust me, you won't be able to handle all his flirting with other girls forever.

Remember, you are who you are. You can't help how you feel. Don't fake it just so that your relationship remains intact. You'll definitely feel unhappy with those circumstances if you do. And when that relationship ends (and it will if you don't put the real you out there) you're bound to feel far more responsible than you actually are. Why? Because you'll fool yourself into believing you have control over him and your relationship as long as you change to fit into his feelings. You don't, so it's best to put the real you out there and date a guy who loves that girl. That relationship will be one that is far more fulfilling than one that is good only on his terms.

So, like I've said from the get-go, it's absolutely essential to follow the Golden Rule. All it means is that you should just be yourself. Then, if a breakup happens, keep in mind that you are a predetermined shape. It takes the pressure off you and switches the responsibility to him. It's not your issue, it's his.

WHEN IT HAPPENS

Now that we've gone through a little breakup psychology les-son, we can discuss an actual breakup and what to do in order to get out alive, dignity intact. During the actual conversation:

- **Listen.** Perhaps what he is saying to you has real merit. He could be telling you that he's simply not ready for a serious relationship but that you are amazing nonetheless. If you aren't listening, you won't hear this ego boost he's attempting to give you.
- **Ask questions.** You have every right to know the reason behind the breakup. Understanding what's going on will allow you to forgive the issue rather than brood over *x*, *y*, and *z* for days on end.
- **Stand up for yourself.** If he starts to criticize you and cites a personal reason for the breakup, stand up for yourself. Don't allow anyone—especially a guy who is ending it—to disrespect you.
- **Speak your mind.** This is your opportunity to bring up anything that's bothered *you* in the relationship. You probably won't get another chance, so do him a favor, too, and let him know what he could have done differently. Maybe he'll take your advice the next time around.
- **Accept it.** If this guy wants to end the relationship, accept it. Just because you want the relationship to work doesn't mean you can force someone to stay who does not want to. Don't embarrass yourself by pleading for another chance from someone who absolutely does not deserve one.

MOVING ON

In order to move on, remember that the breakup is *his* issue, not yours. You're officially free from a relationship that was heading nowhere fast. Now you can get out there and find a better one. Rejoice, sweetness. The grass really is greener on the other side. No matter how bright the future is, though, I do understand it can be a little tricky in the meantime. You've lost a friend, and that is a bummer.

Let's touch on what you must understand to move back into a happier space. Be sure you can answer these questions and feel confident about your responses:

- Was he a Baddie? If he was, why did you date him?
- Did you manipulate your behavior so he would like you? If so, can you acknowledge that you did this and forgive yourself?
- What did you want from the relationship? Did you achieve it?
- What have you learned, and where do you want to go now?

Answering these questions will give you the answers and explanation you are looking for. Even if they're tough, they're necessary. Having these answers will give you closure and allow you to heal and move into better relationships.

You can also taken action, doing different things that will

help you get over the loss of your relationship. First and fore-most, delete his number and e-mail from your cell phone con-tacts. Immediately, you've removed the temptation to commu-nicate with him further, because now you are simply not able to. Soon enough, you won't even want to. Then,

- **Spend a few nights with Mom and Dad.** These are two people who love you unconditionally, even when some toolbag does not. They have a way of making it all better, and you can count on them to deliver some laugh-inducing low blows about your ex.

- **Plan a girls' night.** This seems pretty obvious, but nobody can make you feel better like your girls can. Go all-out with them: Put on a hot outfit, go to a fabulous dinner, and strut around a cool party afterward like you own the room.

- **Find something to do.** That's right. Plan some kind of activity that is certain to take your mind off him. Ride horses, go on a hike, take your kid sister to the library. Whatever it is, just do it. Do not mope around your house for days.

- **Kiss a boy.** Yes, kiss a boy. Enjoy it! It will show you that there are a million other guys out there who are still into you.

- **Stay strong.** Remember that you are a good

person and that you deserve an amazing relationship with a guy. Refer back to your love list, reread part two of this book, or the whole book for that matter. It will help to put things back into perspective for you. Love yourself, and go to others who love you too when you need a helping hand.

THE END

In the quest for a relationship, we all have to start some-
where. I started in high school—a fun, flirtatious firecracker
whose flame refused to be extinguished, despite that I experienced my fair share of blunders. Through these blunders,
though, I realized that maybe deep down I was not capable
of approaching relationships in a carefree way forever and
ever. Frequently, it takes a blunder and the humiliation that
follows to realize that you don't want to make silly mistakes
for the rest of your life.

At some point, everyone's lightbulb turns on. You realize
you are ready to get real and to have the serious relationship
that comes with taking the person *you* are seriously. My light-

bulb definitely went on (otherwise, how could I have written this fabulous guide?), but I'm honestly thankful for the carefree times I had when I was a kid. You must allow yourself to be young and experience all that fun before you are able to see that at some point it feels good to move beyond it.

Coming into yourself, into who you are, is a natural progression. It takes experience, some of it good and some of it bad. Once you are ready, you make the decision to put the real you out there, and you expect a real relationship to go along with who this person is.

And who is this girl? She (you) is good, strong, smart, talented, and desirable. If you don't believe all these amazing factoids about yourself, realize that you are viewing who you are through broken glass, and that's a no-no. You must identify what it is that is holding you back from seeing yourself as you really are: an awesome, hot chick. If something is stopping you, once that "something" is identified it must be crushed, so you can appreciate yourself fully. Once you do this, the happy version of you will definitely shine.

Only happy people have good relationships. Partnerships thrive on good energy, on two actively participating members who bring out the good in each other rather than the bad. Happy people are those who are confident in themselves and who display this person to the world. They believe in themselves, not who they fantasize themselves to be, and are satisfied with the reality. Because it *is* reality: You are who you are, and no matter what color you dye your hair, it will not change the person deep down inside.

You cannot control the essential person you were born to be, but you can be satisfied with this person. Self-love goes a long way and doesn't cost a penny. It comes with a delightful added benefit too: the ability to experience successful relationships. That's why you're reading this book. anyway, right? To learn what it takes to score the sweetie and stay happy with him. I've given you all the tools you need to set out and grab what you've always wanted to experience with guys. It's up to you now. Love yourself, and then you will be able to love your guy in the right way.

Take charge of who you are. Show this person to the world. Not every single person will react to you in the way that you hope, but if you put the real you out there, quite a few people will. At the end of the day, it's all anyone can do, but it's good enough to guarantee you happiness.

Peace, and LOVE,

LO BOSWORTH has starred on the smash
MTV reality television series *Laguna Beach* and
The Hills. A graduate of UCLA, Lo lives in Los
Angeles, California. This is her first book.